D0931594

Documenting Change in the Institutions of Knowledge

WITHDRAWN

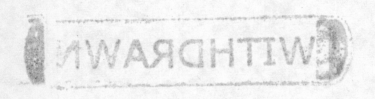

A PROMETHEUS BIBLIOGRAPHY

Documenting Change in the Institutions of Knowledge

Philip C. Ritterbush

Published by **Acropolis Books Ltd.**, Washington, D.C. 20009

THE PROMETHEUS SERIES OF ORIGINAL PAPERBACKS
First Series, 1972

THE BANKRUPTCY OF ACADEMIC POLICY
Peter Caws, S. Dillon Ripley, Philip C. Ritterbush

SCIENTIFIC INSTITUTIONS OF THE FUTURE
AAAS Symposium, December, 1971

TALENT WASTE
How Institutions
of Learning Misdirect Human Resources

© *Copyright 1972 by THOR, Inc.*

Published in cooperation with
THE ARCHIVES OF INSTITUTIONAL CHANGE
Georgetown Office Service Center
3160 O Street, N.W., Washington, D.C. 20007

Editor: Philip C. Ritterbush
Associate Editor: Kathleen S. Paasch
Corresponding Editor: Joan M. Wolfe (Mrs.)
Art Editor: Lenore F. Sams (Mrs.)
Composition: Litho Composition Service
Washington, D.C.

All rights reserved. Except for the inclusion of brief quotations in a review, no part of this book may be reproduced or utilized in any form or by any means, electronic or mechanical, including photocopying, recording or by any information storage and retrieval system, without permission in writing from the publisher.

ACROPOLIS BOOKS LTD.
*Colortone Building, 2400 17th St., N.W.
Washington, D.C. 20009*

Printed in the United States of America by
COLORTONE PRESS, Creative Graphics Inc.
Washington, D.C. 20009¯

Library of Congress Catalog Number 72-3816
Standard Book Number 87491-502-3

Z
7164
.S66R58

Contents

The Institutions of Society

YOUNGSTOWN STATE UNIVERSITY
LIBRARY

322998

"First troops pull out of Cambodia."

IN PREFACE

It is perfectly obvious that a very large number of campus communities are vehemently opposed to President Nixon's responses to the North Vietnamese offensive. The opposition to the bombing of Hanoi and Haiphong was strong and the reaction to the mining of Haiphong harbor will, I believe, be even more widely and deeply felt.

I report these facts not to the people of my campus community, who already know them, but to those outside the university who may still be following the mistaken beliefs that the absence of large scale campus riots in the past two years bespoke either support for or indifference to the conduct of the Vietnam war.

On the contrary, campus revulsion to America's participation in that war is as strong as it has ever been. So, too, is a dangerous and ever growing disenchantment with a political system that has been unable to bring to an end a venture that is now almost universally acknowledged to be immoral at worst, a failure at best.

These facts about the state of the campuses must be of consequence to anyone who is at all concerned with the future health of the American political process for the campuses are no longer unique. Cynicism and despair today among those who will necessarily bear heavy responsibility for running the system tomorrow can only bode ill for the future, and this malaise is spreading steadily through the society.

I do not say these things as spokesman for the Stanford community on the matter of Vietnam. I was not chosen president of Stanford because I was thought to represent anyone else's political views. I hold no one's proxy. Those at Stanford who wish to be heard can each speak for themselves.

I feel a keen responsibility, however, to make known consequences of public policy in and on the university. Since students and faculty have been among the most active of elements in the anti-war movement in the U.S., and because the well-being of universities has been among the chief victims of the war, I feel compelled to bring to public attention the ways on which this nation's involvement in Vietnam affects the institution for which I am responsible.

Richard W. Lyman
President
Stanford University

ILLUSTRATIONS

By Mark Podwal, M.D., of New York City From *The Decline and Fall of the American Empire* (New York: Darien House, 1971), by permission of the artist.

THE ARCHIVES OF INSTITUTIONAL CHANGE

Knowledge is the basis of our wealth, social capacities, and guiding values—the principal treasure of our civilization. We shall all eventually follow in the directions in which it grows and finds applications. While we can neither freely choose nor surely predict its future course, all the major powers of this earth, whether they are corporations, religions, nations, or movements, seek benefits from its advance, whether they want weaponry or wellbeing. Research investments, both public and private, of funds and human talent, have become enormous and now support an extensive complex of institutions: universities, laboratories, academies, libraries, museums, hospitals, and many other kinds of centers. These knowledge institutions, as they might be styled, determine the rate of the advance of knowledge, affect the manner of its application, and, to a lesser and still little understood extent, influence its character and patterns of growth.

Given the consequence of knowledge institutions for the human future, it might be thought that the system would be under continuous study, that decisions about its design and development would be taken with care and all the wisdom that could be brought to bear. But there is no context for such decisions. No public policy reaches the whole complex. Maps have been drawn only of some of its parts. Of the institutions as an entirety there is not even a register or directory. The managers of such institutions seek to respond to financial and intellectual opportunities as they perceive them. This is an accidental process, and one that is competitive, which discourages the institutions from coordinating their efforts among themselves.

In this poor climate for policy, institutional studies have altogether failed to flourish. Another factor is that scholars and scientists would much rather think about the substance of their inquiries than the context in which they occur. Most of the study that institutions have received has been narrowly addressed, so that they are the object of a number of non-communicating specialisms. Along with the other major institutional systems of society, knowledge institutions form part of the subject matter of sociology, and in that field there are some distinguished and highly accomplished students of institutions, although not one who has studied the complex as a whole. The social use of knowledge is a concern that sociologists share with philosophers—of whom few have shown much interest in the establishments actually involved. Anthropologists view institutions as elements of culture, and economists as objects of investment. Students of science policy are concerned with their research functions; educators, with their education functions. From time to time one or another kind of institution is singled out for review: universities by the Carnegie Commission, governmental research by the Hoover Commission, or libraries by another national commission. The fragmentation of knowledge has its counterpart in the professional boundaries observed by various kinds of institutional officers: university business officers, industrial research directors, college personnel directors, professional association executives, or foundation officers, who spend barely any time exploring common concerns.

Although there is a voluminous literature on "organizations," it has only limited applicability to institutions of learning. The concept of organization is intentionally broad; it applies to mechanical systems, all living things, and social entities of all kinds: wherever functional capacities inhere in specialized arrangements. The word institution is derived from *statuere,* to set up. It implies objectives for which a collective enterprise has been constituted, a purpose that unites. Individual institutions are chartered for stated purposes, while the term organization implies the existence of no more than patterns of structure or transactions. Work-flow studies of farmyards and factory floors cannot reach the social and intellectual factors governing the purpose of institutions. Like the illustrations in an anatomy text, the diagrams yielded by organizational studies reveal nothing of the individuality of particular institutions. Here something more akin to biography or the art of portraiture is needed, not only because of the uniqueness of individual institutions, but because they serve to shape and transmit human values—a function which the social sciences have usually excluded from their terms of reference. Culture is the sum of learned behaviors and ideas in human societies; thus institutions might be considered as persisting elements of culture serving socially sanctioned ends. Institutions of learning would be those serving the end of the advancement of knowledge and its application to human concerns. In order to understand them, a sense of the social situation of knowledge must be combined with insights drawn from a range of academic disciplines.

Every institution experiences turnover in members and clients, and must adapt to changing social interests. These and other highly apparent aspects of change, such as growth, need not affect the cultural situation of institutions or the social ends they serve. Institutional change is a structural process that takes place at a deeper level. It is periods of cultural change that expose institutions to the most profound uncertainties, leading to change in their governing objectives and social allegiances. If the cultural mainstream shifts, it will flow toward alternative institutions and leave some traditional establishments high and dry. Knowledge institutions are now encountering demands for change in very fundamental respects, and are undergoing still other changes of which they are barely conscious. Like all historic processes, institutional change takes place in ways that participants must often devote years to come to understand. Are there change agents capable of guiding the destinies of institutions in these complex transitions and what body of knowledge would give them that ability?

Recently the American Academy of Arts and Sciences constituted an Assembly on University Goals and Governance, which reviewed the situation of contemporary universities and concluded that knowledge of a new kind had to be fashioned:

> To improve and reform higher education—not to calm dissidents but to achieve the potentialities of colleges and universities—a kind of knowledge is required that does not now exist. Many in institutions of higher learning are prepared to scrutinize almost everything—the natural environment, government and industry, all manner of other institutions foreign and domestic—but they are loathe to scrutinize themselves and the institutions they inhabit. If reform is not to be mindless, knowledge and data are needed on the character and effects of present educational and research programs. It is essential to know more about how decisions are made and executed in colleges and universities, and how the successes and failures of innovations are communicated so that others may learn from the experiences of those who have experimented with new approaches. Institutional self-study is desirable; it does not suffice for presidents and administrative staff to be interested in such matters. The methods, content, and philosophy of education need to become a more vital interest of many professors, staff, and students. (*A First Report,* Jan 71, p. 7)

The Reference System of the Archives of Institutional Change.

The Archives of Institutional Change is a reference bureau on the cultural and social responses of institutions of learning in America. Its aim is to illuminate the process of institutional change in the world of learning through programs of publication and documentation. It will afford a medium for the exchange of ideas between those studying institutions and policy officers responsible for their welfare.

In order to document the complex process of change, the Archives is undertaking to collect primary sources which may serve as evidence in the future: long-range plans, self-studies, restatements of objectives, and evaluations of individual institutions. No existing documentation center had sought to collect such material. Because such literature is ephemeral and can be collected only while it is still current within the institutions of origin, a new reference center was needed to undertake the task. In order to be selected for the collection, documents must reveal the distinctive objectives or social relationships of an institution, rather than its routine activities or continuing programs. Program materials such as annual reports or college catalogues will be included only where they are the best available evidence for important innovations. Studies and commentaries are the other major component of the collection, ranging from histories of single institutions to theoretical works on the broad social functions that institutions serve.

In order to facilitate comparisions of institutions and demonstrate their relationship to social needs, the Archives employs a distinctive reference system with the following features. A small core library is being formed for works of general significance to institutional change in the world of learning. Within the space of a few years this will result in a highly selective checklist of important publications which serve to define the process of institutional change and the social context within which it occurs. In addition to works of general significance there are general-purpose institutions and works which are best classified under a general heading, so this has been made the first of a series of ten categories which classify not only individual institutions but institutional systems and the social functions they serve. For example, the Bell Telephone Laboratories comprise a single technological institution. The technical university or industrial research center is a generic institution. Technology is itself the broad societal institution which these others subserve. Institutional change may take place through reorientation of a single institution, modification of the generic institution, redirection of the social function of technology, or all of these. Consequently the reference system must be able to accommodate and help to distinguish among works which deal with these different institutional levels. This is the central design feature of the Archives of Institutional Change, as indicated in the accompanying table, which sets out the system of classification.

If a work is deemed to have general significance it is numbered below one thousand (and its first digit does not conform to the rest of the scheme). If it deals with a broad societal institution such as medicine it is numbered in the thousands and the first digit indicates the function, such as human and environmental wellbeing (6). If it documents the objectives or programs of one particular hospital it is given a six-digit number, whose first digit is that of the numerical category, followed by the five digits of its postal "zip code." In the physical arrangement of the collection and in the published bibliographies and other works of reference this serves to group together works on broad societal institutions, generic institutions or groups of institutions, and individual institutions serving the same social function.

The Prometheus Series of Policy Studies.

The Archives publishes a series of policy studies under the series title "Prometheus," featuring reviews and abstracts of its literature holdings. The first series, published during 1971 and 1972, was undertaken to demonstrate that the policies of individual institutions have significant effects on the social situation of knowledge. *The Bankruptcy of Academic Policy* criticized universities for failing to define their objectives, which precludes the pursuit of rational policies, and recommended approaches to the evolution of institutional policies. *Scientific Institutions of the Future* described the changes that various kinds of scientific

TABLE   Reference System

Works of General Significance (numbered in hundreds)	Broad Societal Institution (numbered in thousands)	Generic Institution (numbered in ten thousands)
000-Census, directories	1000-Universalization of knowledge	10000-Institutions of elementary, secondary, and popular education
100-Journals, periodicals	2000-Higher education and research	20000-Institutions of higher education and research
200-History of institutions	3000-Technology, communications	30000-Technological and communications institutions
300-Inter-relations of institutions	4000-Economic functions of society	40000 Corporations, other economic institutions
400-Social relations of unstitutions	5000-Human service, community development	50000-Human service institutions and professions
500-Appraisals of institutions	6000-Human and environmental wellbeing	60000-Institutions for health and environmental protection
600-Institutional change and alternative institutions	7000-Governing, public policy	70000-Governmental and civic institutions
700-Policy, planning, and institutional objectives	8000-Science	80000-Scientific institutions
800-Human values within institutions	9000-Culture, art, religion, philosophy	90000-Cultural, art, religious, philosophical institutions
900-Management, administration, organizational behavior		
0000-General functions of society		
00000-General-purpose institutions		

research establishments will have to make in order to fulfill social expectations. *Talent Waste: How Institutions of Learning Misdirect Human Resources* showed how the lack of coherent human resource policies within institutions has led to a surplus of academically trained specialists that coincides with a shortage of talented individuals needed to address contemporary social problems. *Documenting Change in the Institutions of Knowledge: A Prometheus Bibliography* provides a cumulative listing of the abstracts of entries in the Archives of Institutional Change during the same period, including those published as digests of literature in each of the previous titles and two test issues.

The second series of "Prometheus" publications will be devoted to profiles of change occuring in specific institutional contexts: off-campus study, information technology, biomedical research and health care, the role of the humanities in technical establishments, and the role of intellectual institutions in solving contemporary problems. Each of these studies will compare mainstream institutions with alternative institutions, gauge their vitality, and estimate the degree of change that seems necessary in order to fulfill public expectations and respond to intellectual opportunity.

The "Prometheus" series offers a new outlet for informed, constructive criticism of our knowledge institutions. Concerned citizens, students, and members of institutions of learning may find it a means of ready access to viewpoints and sources within the full range of academic disciplines bearing upon the policies of our institutions of learning and their social responses. As the series develops, it will become a rich reference resource on the changes underway throughout the institutional realm to which it is devoted. Policy officers of institutions, who rarely have time for exploratory reading, may find it a valuable set of summaries of institutional issues—bringing together knowledgeable views, proposals for change, reviews, and summaries of wide expanses of literature that would otherwise be inaccessible to them. The policy focus of "Prometheus" is one of its most distinctive features, setting it apart from educational research information systems, for example, and necessitating a broad interdisciplinary approach. Nor is it simply a register of opinion. Its aim is to summarize and contribute to knowledge of institutions which has a likely bearing on policies—their own and those of public authorities.

The "Prometheus" series is published by Acropolis Books of Washington, D.C., Alphons Hackl, Publisher. They are available from the Archives by subscription ($25.00 per series of six titles; $20.00 for additional series purchases), by standing order for future titles, and by individual title ($4.35 each, including postage and handling). Individuals willing to serve as Correspondents of the Archives, who send documents and suggestions for future publications, may subscribe for $20.00 per year.

The Archives is organized as a nonprofit corporation under a board of directors. Its collection is presently housed in Washington, D.C. Its advisory board brings a wide range of experience in educational innovation, reference systems, and policy studies. Its members are Lynton K. Caldwell, Professor of Government at Indiana University, and author of *Science, Technology, and Public Policy: A Bibliography;* Maurice Goldsmith, Director of The Science Policy Foundation of London. Bernard Karpel, Librarian of the Museum of Modern Art; Howard J. Lewis, Director of Information, National Academy of Sciences, and Editor of the Newsletter of the Science and Public Policy Study Group; Russell Shank, Director of Libraries of the Smithsonian Institution; Edward Shils of the Committee on Social Thought of the University of Chicago and Editor of *Minerva;* and Goodwin Watson, Associate Director of the Union of Experimenting Colleges and Universities.

Future "Prometheus" publications will in general have guest advisory editors who will help to commission articles and reviews as well as select titles and documents to be included in the Archives. The series editor and director of the Archives is Philip C. Ritterbush, a cultural historian who has been studying institutional aspects of science, higher education, and the arts since 1961, and has also served in a number of policy analysis assignments, in the Office of Science and Technology, the U.S. Senate, and the Smithsonian Institution. He has served as an editor or consultant with the Yale University Press, the White House Conference on Youth, the American Association for the Advancement of Science, *The Saturday Review—Science,* and the Academy for Contemporary Problems.

INSTITUTION AS A SOCIAL CONCEPT, A REVIEW ESSAY.

James K. Feibleman, *The Institutions of Society* (310)
(N.Y.: Humanities Press, reprinted 1968), 400 pp., $10.00.

Institutions are more enduring than social groups and embrace much more. They are the elements of which cultures are composed. Perhaps it is their situation in between the small group and the culture as a whole that has allowed them to escape systematic analysis. Rather than face-to-face encounter, by which groups take decisions, or the elaboration of distinctive traits, by which cultures manifest themselves, institutions achieve their effects by shaping attitudes and providing a milieu where tasks of certain kinds may be undertaken. They are usually so well integrated with their parent culture as to become almost invisible against its background, while to those within them, whom they so deeply influence, they often appear to be a neutral setting for individual actions—merely a stage on which life's drama develops at will. It has been our habit of thought to attribute social values to the culture as a whole, although they are borne by its institutions, and to credit ourselves as individuals with accomplishments which only institutions make possible. It is as though one had a map of a city and a sampling of its inhabitants, but ignored the individual streets, buildings, plazas, and utility systems of which it is composed. But these are the very center of the urban experience, where, in Churchill's epigram, there operates that vital dialectic whereby we shape our buildings and our buildings in turn reshape those who dwell among them. What we have risked losing, through our ignorance of the institutional middle ground of human experience, is the capacity to nurture desirable cultural values, to solve social problems, and to achieve humane settings for our life efforts.

"What motivates society in the main is the problems it cannot solve." (p. 178) Institutions are constituted to promulgate answers to social needs—service institutions to supply food, clothing, sexual satisfaction, and shelter, higher institutions to satisfy curiosity or the longing for community. They are certain ways of using tools established by social groups—a direct counterpart in advanced societies of the tools which are the focus of man's environmental relations in settings which are less elaborate socially or economically. Through the elaborate process of institutionalization, collective efforts at problem-solving take concrete form. Service institutions include the family, transportation, communication, economics, practical technologies, education, the state, the military, and the law. Higher institutions, which furnish purposes to the others, include the sciences, the arts, philosophy, and religion. Feibleman suggests that this hierarchy of institutions should generate values, diffuse them, and apply them in service to society. At the top of the hierarchy is "the leading institution," that which is re-garded as most important by a given society. In ancient China it was the family; in medieval Europe it was the church; in today's America it is the business cor-poration.

All institutions have four elements: personnel, organization, equipment, and procedures. In the context of operation each of these serves the central purpose of the institution. Personnel observe and help to perpetuate the institution's *myth* of its origins or character. "No good member of an institution ever regarded the myth of that institution as anything except a flat statement of the truth. It is only from the outside and with the advantage of a distant and foreign perspec-tive that the myth of an institution ever appears otherwise. . . . Thus the effects upon individuals of the institution which they serve might lie deeper than they know and reach further than they suspect." (p. 169) The organization of an in-stitution is based upon its *"charter,"* Malinowski's term for its collective purpose. "As the specific doctrine of the institution the charter stands for the abstract ideas on which it rests." (p. 175) The equipment of the institutions symbolizes its functions and sometimes finds employment exclusively as *symbols*: as in the judge's robe or the professor's gown. "When we consider that artifacts lead lives of their own and that they also have effects upon their makers, it is possible to see how complex the situation becomes." (p. 171) Finally, the procedures of the institution manifest themselves in the quality of *style*. "Style is the precise fashion chosen for behaving, the correct way of doing things. It is how the members of an institution use their symbols in accordance with ways called for by the myth." (p. 172)

The leading institution has profound effects upon the society as a whole, for its myth becomes the ethos of the entire society. Its charter becomes the *eidos*—the system of ideas characterizing the society. Its symbols generate the *basic value system*. And its style is widely imposed through a basic process of *authority* which is rarely questioned and which hardly ever needs to be sustained with physical force. (pp. 228-242) The leading institution is in Feibleman's view simply a paradigm case for the cultural effects of institutions as a whole. Thus Fiebleman successfully relates individuals, groups, institutions, cultures, and society, as components of an interacting system, identifying the manner in which they interact and recognizing the very ample role of institutions.

Objects oftentimes "get away from us" (as have autos and handguns, for example) and gain an unwanted influence; Feibleman styles this the "alienation of the artifact." (p. 121) So, too, may institutions fall away from their once-governing purposes. For one thing they embody conservative tendencies and may very readily become ends in themselves, obstacles to the needs they were meant to satisfy, and dominating influences over the individuals they were intended to serve. As institutions become alienated from their original purposes, they become more and more concerned with their own growth and survival as ends in themselves. An institution dominated by these secondary purposes subverts its charter in order to grow or to survive in the face of threat to its existence. Another factor in the alienation of institutions is the existence of a menagerial cadre which is not engaged in the primary productive endeavor of institutions but in their administrative activities. Rather than regard their function as the enhancement of members' efforts, such managers engage in inappropriate and obstructive institutional politics. The end result is to degrade the character of institutions and frustrate the needs of society.

> It is in the hubris of institutions that the truth of the Frankenstein myth becomes relevant. The monster that man makes which he can no longer control is nothing if not the institution. . . .The tendency of institutions to grow continues long after they have fulfilled their specific and proper function, and drags along with them all those who have been committed to their cause. . . . The institution which can only do what it has been doing is not doing enough. Novelty is life, and we expect of an institution that it will progress, progress not necessarily in the direction of size but in the direction of development, of the discovery or introduction of new ideas, new values, new actions. When it can no longer fulfill this requirement it fails so to speak as an institution, and this means the beginning of a decline. A simpler way to put this perhaps would be to say that institutions decline and often even die when they can no longer do their job. (p. 311)

Here we have a prescient explanation of the pathology of institutions, which has become such a significant concern over the years since this book was written.

"The control of institutions must await the understanding of institutions," Feibleman observes. (p. 372) In the face of this unarguable proposition contemporary America prefers ignorance, *ad hoc* regulation in a welter of inappropriate legal stragegms, anxious defensive rhetoric from institutional leaders, and mounting impatience on the part of a minority intent on reform. The longer this situation persists the deeper the damage will go, and more will maintain that all institutions are bad in themselves.

Feibleman anticipates the contemporary humanistic outlook by arguing that in the final state of the process of institutionalization all mankind becomes an institution, and that the entire enterprise of philosophy is a search for the charter that would establish that end. There would no longer be a leading institution. Instead a harmonious interplay would occur. Freed from the anxious condition of over-belief, institutions could live comfortably with limited truths. "That we do not have such a situation now, it is hardly necessary to add. The alternation of institutions in power in actual societies is a jockeying for position in the effort to seek out and satisfy the ideal of the natural society. It is culture, working on the trial-and-error method. We have our planned societies, using the term, societies, here in the narrow sense of nations or states. But we do not yet have and we never have had a planned culture. We have not yet learned how to step back from the problem with the necessary detachment in order to pause and consider what institutions there could be, in addition to those that there are. Do we, for instance, have exactly the institutions we want and in the shape we want them? Such a venture lies far in the future, yet no doubt it represents the aim of ultimate rationality. In terms of it, as might be expected, we shall build better than we know, but at the present time the ideal of the planned culture is far beyond our powers, and even almost beyond our understanding." (pp. 358-359)

Feibleman suggests that natural or primitive society would yield the best available insights into the attainment of a planned culture—one better adjusted to its physical environment than our own (as he urges in another passage remarkably sensitive to an issue that would not come to general notice for another ten years). To heal our social ills we need more than a new therapeutic routine. The task requires knowledge of a new kind and a logic of values—to which *The Institutions of Society* makes a most worthy and nearly unprecedented contribution.

0. General Works

CENSUS, DIRECTORIES

Federal R&D Installations.

National Science Foundation, *Directory of Federal R&D Installations for the Year Ending June 30, 1969* (001) NSF 70-23 (Washington: U.S. Government Printing Office) 1044 pp., $6.75. A Report to the Federal Council for Science and Technology. The first major compilation of the array of resources in the government's intramural laboratories, excluding classified installations and contract centers of the Department of Health, Education, and Welfare. Seven hundred twenty-three installations are included, with information as to the contractor (if any), director, address, personnel, funding, major functions and activities, and publication references. This extensive complex is comparable in size to the entire domain of university research and development in science and technology. The publication of this directory should be regarded as an invitation to compare the academic and governmental subsystems within the overall system of research institutions.

International Directory of Science Policymaking Bodies.

UNESCO, *World Directory of National Science Policy-Making Bodies* (002), three volumes (1966-68). Available from the UNESCO Publications Center, P.O. Box 433, New York, New York 10016.

Museums.

American Association of Museums, *The Official Museum Directory 1971* (003) (New York: Crowell-Collier Educational Corporation, 1971) 1022 pp. $35.00 Available from The Official Museum Directory, P.O. Box 4857, Washington, D.C. 20007. Six thousand museums and related institutions are listed state-by-state and for Canada, reflecting the addition of seven such institutions for each week since the last edition in 1965. Each listing covers staff and organization, activities, publications, hours, and membership. In subsequent sections museums are listed alphabetically, their personnel are listed alphabetically, and museums are classified by category. An invaluable reference work which has successfully overcome the difficulties posed by the diversity of the institutions included.

Associations.

Margaret Fisk, ed., *Encyclopedia of Associations* (004), 6th ed. (Detroit, Mich.: Gale Research Co., 1970), 1468 pp., $32.50. Listing by 19 broad categories, alphabetically by key word, of more than 15,000 trade associations, professional societies, labor unions, fraternal and patriotic organizations, and other voluntary groups.

National Service.
National Service Secretariat, *Directory of Service Organizations* (005) (Washington, D.C., 1968). Suggests to young people how they may identify agencies with which they might serve. Special mention is given to the National Register of Volunteer Jobs in Court Settings, Boulder County Juvenile Court, Boulder, Colorado 80302.

Publishing.
Literary Market Place with Names & Numbers, 1972-1972 Edition (006) (New York: R. R. Bowker Co., 1972) xii + 649 pp. Addresses and listings of senior staff for publishers, magazines, and a diverse array of other kinds of entities, eighty-two in all.

Social Change Organizations, Directory.
Alternatives Foundation, *Directory of Social Change* (007), 1526 Gravenstein Highway North, Sebastopol, California 97452. Published 1969. $1.00 Listing of about 400 social change agencies in the U.S. and Canada.

Physical Sciences, Engineering.
National Referral Center, *Physical Sciences, Engineering, A Directory of Information Resources in the United States* (008) (Washington, D.C.: Library of Congress, Science and Technology Division, 1971) iii + 803 pp. Available from the Superintendent of Documents for $6.50. Listing of 2891 information or reference establishments in alphabetical order, accompanied by subject index.

Federal Government.
National Referral Center for Science and Technology, *A Directory of Information Resources in the United States Federal Government* (009) (Washington, D.C.: Library of Congress, June 67), vii + 411 pp. From the Superintendent of Documents, $2.75.

Environmental Research.
State University College at Fredonia, New York, *Directory of Organizations Concerned with Environmental Research* (010) (January, 1970), 150 pp., $2.00. From the SUNY College of Fredonia, N.Y. 14063.

A Model Institutional Inventory.
Policy Institute, Syracuse University Research Corporation, Merrill Lane, University Heights, Syracuse, N.Y. 13210, *Environmental Research Laboratories in the Federal Government* (011), 2 vols., Sept. 71, 973 pp., $20.00. This important institutional survey goes well beyond the Federal Government's previous catalogue, National Science Foundation, *Directory*

of Federal R&D Installations for the Year Ending June 30, 1969 (001) , available as NSF 70-23 from the U.S. Government Printing Office, $6.75. In addition to standard information previously available, this new inventory lists publications, physical facilities, training programs, and a list of meetings for 170 laboratories, arranged by parent agency. Historical budget data and a concise statement of institutional history are given. What is most valuable, however, are breakdowns of professional staff by field, and interpretive descriptions of unusual equipment or facilities, institutional ties, and future plans. It is probably necessary for a critical field investigator to report on these matters, as Albert Teich has done to good effect in this compilation, rather than to rely on the institutions themselves for such statements. The summary data on each laboratory apply to all its programs, not just to environmental research, to which the Argonne National Laboratory, for example, devotes only a portion of its effort. It is very difficult for establishments to classify their efforts into categories other than those governing their operation. This catalogue offsets that disadvantage by appending environmental research program statements to some of the entries. What would seem to be even more desirable would be a periodic census of research establishments, governmental, industrial, academic, and independent, in a number of topical areas of strong national concern. The usefulness of this catalogue would be vastly enhanced if it included these other institutional domains. The failure of the Federal Government to support a periodic census of the world of learning reveals a fondness for ignorance of institutional arrangements—an avoidance of data gathering that might lead to confrontations with the inadequacies of present-day policy.

Societies.
National Academy of Sciences, 2101 Constitution Avenue, N.W., Washington, D.C. 20418. *Scientific, Technical and Related Societies of the United States,* 9th ed. (012) 1971, 213 pp., $13.50. Alphabetical listing of 551 membership societies devoted to particular scientific, engineering, and other technical disciplines and professions.

Physics and Astronomy.
American Institute of Physics, 335 East 45th Street, New York, N.Y. 10017, *Graduate Programs in Physics and Astronomy; A Handbook for Advisors of Prospective Doctoral and Master's Students* (013) , 1968, xxii, 437 pp. $5.00. Listings of 163 Ph.D. and 256 Master's programs in physics, and 34 Ph.D. and 34 Master's programs in astronomy, most with faculty biodata, research areas, and student requirements.

Engineering Societies.
Engineers Joint Council, 345 E. 47th Street, New York, N.Y. 10017, *Directory of Engineering Societies and Related Organizations* (014) 1970, 252 pp., $8.00. Listing, principally by state, of 318 organizations.

Graduate Schools.
Herbert B. Livesey and Gene A. Robbins, *Guide to American Graduate Schools,* 2nd ed. (015) (N.Y.: Viking Press, 1970), xxxviii, 410 pp. $12.95. Analysis of 643 institutions, listed alphabetically with descriptions of each graduate program or division listing fields of study, degrees offered, number of full-time and part-time students, requirements, admission and tuition information, and number of faculty. The index to fields of study may be used to locate institutions offering particular subjects. Another valuable feature is the listing of associated research facilities and special programs at some institutions. For ampler narrative listings of Ph.D. (only) programs see Robert Quick, ed., *A Guide to Graduate Study,* published by the American Council on Education.

Independent Research Laboratories.
Union Internationale du Laboratoires Independants, Ashbourne House, Alberon Gardens, London, N.W. 11 OBN, England. *Register of Members, 1971* (016) 217 pp., $3.00. Listing by nation of 135 independent consulting firms and private laboratories.

Conservation.
National Wildlife Federation, 1412 16th Street, N.W., Washington, D.C. 20036, *Conservation Directory 1972; A Listing of Organizations, Agencies, and Officials Concerned with Natural Resource Use and Management* (017) vii, 152 pp., $2.00. Listing of about 70 U.S. Government agencies, over 200 organizations and commissions, and over 300 state agencies and associations, giving staff lists, concise statement of purpose, address, and titles of publications.

Higher Education.
National Center for Educational Statistics, U.S. Office of Education, OE-5000-71, *Education Directory; Higher Education; 1970-71* (018) xxv, 515 pp. Alphabetical listing, by state, of 2,573 accredited institutions of higher education offering at least two-year post-secondary education programs, including address and zip code, principal officers, FICE code, enrollment, calendar system, and control or affiliation, as of 15 Sept 70.

Hospitals.
American Hospital Association, 840 North Lake Shore Drive, Chicago, Illinois 60611. *Hospitals, Guide Issue* (019) 1 Aug 71, 620 pp., $7.50.

Listings of hospitals, members of The American Hospital Association, international/national/regional health organizations, national health agencies, state/provincial organizations, and educational programs, followed by hospital statistics, buyers' guides, and indices.

Mental Health

National Clearinghouse for Mental Health Information, Public Health Service Publ. 1268, *Mental Health Directory 1971* (020). U.S. Gov't Printing Office, 1971, 1724-0136, vii, 480 pp., $3.75. Listing by state of over 3,000 centers classified as psychiatric hospitals, general hospitals with separate psychiatric services, residential centers for emotionally disturbed children, outpatient mental health clinics, mental health day/night facilities, community mental health centers, transitional mental health facilities, other multiservice mental health facilities, and components in other facilities, giving addresses and descriptions of services provided. Listing of other directories, pp. 478-480.

Information.

Anthony T. Kruzas, ed., *Encyclopedia of Information Systems and Services* (021) (Ann Arbor, Mich.: Edwards Brothers, 1971) xii, 1109 pp., $67.50. Over 800 organizations are listed in alphabetical sequence. The subtitle of the volume indicates something of its scope: "A guide to information centers, computerized systems and services, networks and cooperative programs, data banks, documentation centers, information storage and retrieval systems, micrographic systems and services, research centers and projects, clearinghouses and referral centers, coordinating agencies, consulting and planning services, information offices, industrial research information centers, professional associations, and specialized library reference services." The standard entry format is name, date established, other sponsoring organizations, director, staff, system or service description, scope, input sources, holdings, serial publications, non-serial publications, microform services, magnetic tape services, other services, equipment, user equipment requirements, user restrictions, and addenda. Twelve indices are provided: alphabetic, names, subject, abstracting and indexing services, computer applications and services, data collection and analysis centers, micrographic applications and services, networks and cooperative programs, research, selective dissemination systems, and serial publications. A noteworthy publication on a rapidly changing institutional universe.

Trade and Professional Associations.

Craig Colgate, Jr., ed., *1971 National Trade and Professional Associations of the United States* (022) (Washington, D.C.: Columbia Books, 1971) 320 pp., $12.50. Alphabetical listing of more than 4,300 national associations.

Research Establishments.
Archie M. Palmer, *Research Centers Directory, 3rd ed.* (023) (Detroit, Mich.: Gale Research Company, 1968) 884 pp., $39.50. Contains 4,500 entries arranged alphabetically in sixteen categories, as follows: agriculture, home economics, and nutrition; astronomy; business, economics, and transportation; conservation; education; engineering and technology; government and public affairs; labor and industrial relations; law; life sciences; mathematics; physical and earth sciences; regional and area studies; social sciences, humanities, and religion; multidisciplinary programs; and research coordinating offices. Indices for personal names, subjects, center names, and parent institutions.

Chemistry.
American Chemical Society, Special Issue Sales, 1155 16th Street, N.W., Washington, D.C. 20036. *Directory of Graduate Research 1971* (024) xx, 796 pp. $15.00. Listings under chemistry, chemical engineering, biochemistry, and pharmaceutical and/or medicinal chemistry of faculty bio-bibliographies and research interests, candidates completing doctorates (with dissertation titles), postdoctoral investigators, and interdisciplinary programs of North American academic departments awarding the Ph.D.

International Scientific Organizations.
Organization for Economic Cooperation and Development, *Organisations scientifiques internationales* (025) (Paris: O.C.D.E., 1965) 287 pp. Available from the Publications Office, O.C.D.E., 2 rue Andre-Pascal, Paris XVI.

Private Foundations.
Marianna O. Lewis, editor, *The Foundation Directory.* Edition 4 (026) Prepared by the Foundation Center (Columbia University Press, 1971) xviii + 642 pp., listing by state of 5,454 private foundations. $15.00 direct order price.

Engineering.
American Society for Engineering Education, *Engineering College Research and Graduate Study* (027), Supplement to *Engineering Education,* Vol. 62, no. 6 (1972), pp. 563-769. $7.00 from the Society, One Dupont Circle, N.W., Washington, D.C. 20036.

Urban Studies.
Grace M. Taher, ed., *University Urban Research Centers* (028) 2nd ed., The Urban Institute, 2100 M. Street, N.W., Washington, D.C. 20037 (1971), 299 pp., $2.75. Approximately 300 centers listed alphabetically by state.

National Black Organizations.
Directory (029), compiled by AFRAM Associates, Inc.. 68-72 East 131st Street, Harlem, N.Y. 10037. 111 pp., $5.00. Lists over 150 organizations which exist primarily for the purpose of aiding the lives and fostering the interests of black people, in eight categories: economic and business, educational, religious, fraternal, professional/occupational, political, civic, and foundations.

JOURNALS, PERIODICALS

Minerva: A Review of Science, Learning, and Policy.
(100) Editor, Edward Shils, c/o Macmillan Journals Ltd., 4 Little Essex Street, London WC2R 3LF, England. Quarterly. Annual subscription, $10.50 payable by dollar check to Macmillan Journals Ltd., Brunel Road, Basingstoke, Hampshire, England. The leading serious journal on national policies in higher education and research.

Change.
(101) Issued ten times yearly. George W. Bonham, Editor-in-Chief. Subscriptions, $10.00 per year in the U.S. and Canada, $11.50 elsewhere; P.O. Box 2450, Boulder, Colorado 80302. The most important outlet for writing on the process of change in higher education.

The Chronicle of Higher Education.
(102) Editor, Corbin Gwaltney. 38 issues per year, annual rate $20.00; foreign and classroom rates on request. 1717 Massachusetts Avenue, N.W., Washington, D.C. 20036. Weekly newspaper on higher education. Information and rates on microfilm of back issues from University Microfilms, Ann Arbor, Michigan 48106.

Higher Education.
(103) American member of Editorial Board, Dr. Robert O. Berdahl, State University of New York, Buffalo, N.Y. Quarterly, subscriptions at 40 Dfl for individuals and 70 Dfl for institutions from Elsevier Publishing Company, Box 211, Amsterdam, The Netherlands. An international journal of higher education and educational planning.

Research Policy, Research Management, and Planning.
Research Policy (104) . A new quarterly journal, published by Elsevier's North-Holland Publishing Company, Journal Division, Post Office Box 211, Amsterdam, The Netherlands. Edited by C. Freeman and T.C. Sinclair of the Science Policy Research Unit at the University of Sussex and H. Krauch and R. Coenen at the Studiengruppe fur Systemforschung, Bergstrasse 143, 69 Heidelberg, Germany. "In industrial research

nowadays the main problem is not how to manage research, but how to determine its appropriate volume and scope, how to bring it in line with the long-term planning of the company and how to integrate it with other operations. In government research policy, the key question is how to determine priorities. Increasing social concern with the short- and long-term consequencies of scientific research and technical innovation has led to a rapid growth of interest in policy for research. It also has led to a growing need to relate the private decisions of the individual researcher, laboratory, or firm to a wider social context in which the full social costs and benefits of an innovation may find expression. . . . The experiences of innovating organizations in attempting, planning, and implementing various innovations, whether complex or simple, are relatively little known or studied. The literature which deals with these questions and other problems of research and development policy is relatively unstructured and scattered in the journals of many different disciplines. RESEARCH POLICY provides a focus for this literature and the policy debate it evokes." Annual rate Dfl 91.00 or $26.00. The first issue, November, 1971, included articles on program appraisal, research priorities, and technological forecasting.

Integration of Knowledge.
Center for Integrative Education, *Main Currents in Modern Thought* (105) Issued five times yearly. Subscriptions, $6.50 to individuals, $14.50 to institutions, foreign add $.50 postage; from the Center, 12 Church St., New Rochelle, New York 10805. "Its editors assume that the laws of nature and of man as formulated by science, the universals of philosophy and the principles of art, as well as the truths of comparative religion, can be orchestrated into a harmonious, meaningful, ethically compelling body of teachings which can and should be made the central core of study in the educative process at all levels."

Social Policy.
(106) bimonthly, Frank Riessman, editor. Subscription rate, $8.00; students, $6.00. 184 Fifth Avenue, Suite 500, New York, New York 10010. A general magazine dedicated to structural change in society, serving also as a point of exchange for workshops, seminars, and "theory collectives."

INNOVATION.
(107) Monthly magazine for professional "managers of business and other organizations who must deal with the intense social and technical change characteristic of a society shaped by technology." Editor, Michael F. Wolff. Annual subscriptions, $45.00 in North America, $55.00 elsewhere. Published for members of The Innovation Group, Ford Park, Executive Director. 265 Madison Avenue, New York, N.Y. 10016.

YOUNGSTOWN STATE UNIVERSITY 322998
LIBRARY

Daedalus.
(108) Editor, Stephen R. Graubard, American Academy of Arts and Sciences, 7 Linden Street, Cambridge, Mass. 02138. Quarterly, subscriptions at $8.00 in U.S., $8.50 elsewhere, from the Academy, 280 Newton Street, Brookline, Mass. 02146. One of the best general publications on the world of learning, its social involvements, and the processes of change resulting from the changing character of knowledge.

The Public Interest.
(109) Editors, Irving Kristol and Daniel Bell, 10 East 53rd Street, New York, New York 10022. Subscriptions $7.50, add $1.00 foreign, from Box 542, Old Chelsea, New York, New York 10011. From the prospectus: "The Public Interest is not some kind of pre-existing platonic idea; rather, it emerges out of differences of opinion, reasonably propounded."

Harvard Educational Review.
(110) Quarterly. Longfellow Hall, 13 Appian Way, Cambridge, Mass. 02138. Subscriptions $10.00 per year, $11.00 in Canada, and $12.00 elsewhere, from Subscriber Service Department, 106 Tenth Street, Des Moines, Iowa 50305.

AERA. American Educational Research Journal.
(111) Editor, Richard L. Turner, School of Education, Room 229, Indiana University, Bloomington, Indiana 47401. Quarterly, subscriptions $8.00, from 1126 16th Street, N.W., Washington, D.C. 20036.

Review of Educational Research.
(112) Editor, Samuel Messick, Box 2604, Educational Testing Service, Princeton, N.J. 08540. Quarterly, subscriptions $10.00 from 1126 16th Street, N.W., Washington, D.C. 20036.

HISTORY OF INSTITUTIONS

Technics—an Abuse of Reason.
Lewis Mumford, "The Myth of the Machine," *The Pentagon of Power* (200) (N.Y.: Harcourt Brace Jovanovich, 1970) vi + 496 pp., $12.95. History of the subordination of humane elements of western civilization to power motives, recounted in the development of large-scale technology.

The Triumph of Academic Values.
Christopher Jencks and David Riesman, *The Academic Revolution* (201) (New

York: Doubleday, 1968) xx + 544 pp. and references; paper, $4.95 (Doubleday Anchor Books). Jencks and Riesman have attempted a sociological and historical analysis of American higher education, aiming to define the relationship between higher education and American society. Their analysis covers all types of academic institutions and the interest groups to which they cater. They discuss generational conflict, social mobility, professional schools, public vs. private colleges, geographic interest groups, coeducational and women's schools, sectarian colleges, ethnic colleges, community colleges, experimental colleges, and graduate schools. The title, *The Academic Revolution,* refers to the rise to power of the academic professions, the redistribution of power within the university through the increased professionalism of the faculty. The authors claim that the universities have become "pacesetters" in promoting meritocratic values: that they choose both faculty and students on the basis of "output" or ability to do "good academic work," rather than on class or ethnic background, age, sex, or religion. Institutions of higher education have great influence on other institutions and on the larger society because they foster the dissemination of meritocratic values. They believe that special-interest colleges do little to shape the future and will eventually give way entirely to the university college, which will continue the trend toward meritocracy.

The Refusal to Define the University— A Characteristic American Failing.
Laurence R. Veysey, *The Emergence of the American University* (202) (University of Chicago Press, 1965) xiv, 505 pp. $10.00, paper (1970), $3.95. Following a period of reform that established it as a stable institution in the 1890s, the American university gained wealth and social status partly as a result of maintaining even among its own members a systematic incomprehension of its purposes and allegiances, according to this sensitive and well documented interpretation. Since then its departmental structure and administrative routines have become fixed, as it was in that decade that diversity of educational programs was forsaken in the competition for growth that has continued ever since. "Few new ideas have been advanced on the purpose of higher education since 1900, and there have also been few deviations in its basic pattern of administration." (p.338) Differences of aim and values were concealed by a nearly universal unwillingness to unmask a central myth, that formal education constituted a remedy for the important problems faced by society. "As one glances over the whole range of academic structure which had developed, noting the disparity of the motives which cemented it from top to bottom, it is difficult to avoid concluding that the institution would have fallen apart had not this powerful optimistic myth captured the minds of its middle ranks." (pp.336-37)

Our sense of novelty in the contemporary plight of the university may not survive Veysey's account of a student commune in shacks near Stanford that were torn down in 1902, the refusal by Harvard students of an offer of self government in 1907, student-faculty estrangement revealed by two nineteenth-century murders of professors by students, or the long-standing habit of regarding students as a disloyal subject population. When faculties sought influence over the conditions of their professional existence, sober critics deplored "revolt" in the university. Sixty years before the specter of the multiversity the variousness of the undertakings of the University of Chicago led it to be called "Harper's Bazaar" in a pun on the name of its first president. New rational methods of university administration were called for in the 1880s and a decade later there was a flourishing black market in themes.

The historian can find scarcely any record of reasons for decisions in the formative decade of the 1890s, because institutional leaders did not give voice to their guiding assumptions. There has been only a steady trend away from "sharp-edge thinking."

Veysey offers a penetrating insight into the vision of the men who created our major intellectual institutions, which says a great deal about their failure to formulate conscious policies: "It involves the act of seeing, stretched forth as it were on a gigantic canvas, a huge network of lines, arranged with order and precision (and yet with fascinating variety) into an aesthetically pleasing shape, like the out-of-scale maps one sometimes sees in railroad timetables. The lines here represent the invisible relations between the units of a sprawling organization. Some are darker, some fainter; some solid, some subtly dotted. To place these lines correctly and with flair requires the hand of an artist. That artist is the creative administrator." (p.369)

Loss of Relevance in Social Studies.
Ernest Becker, *The Lost Science of Man* (203) (N.Y.: George Braziller, 1971) 177 pp., $6.95. Over seventy years ago pioneers in the development of social studies in America, Albion W. Small in sociology and Franz Boas in anthropology, sought to orient these fields toward the solution of social problems. These aspirations were displaced by attempts to impose high standards of quantitative accuracy in these fields. Becker calls for a re-orientation of social science disciplines toward the needs of the human community.

Institutions in the Life of Science.
J.G. Crowther, *Fifty Years with Science* (204) (London: Barrie & Jenkins, 1970, distributed in the U.S. by Humanities Press), 348 pp., $11.00. An observer who credits institutions with a major role in twentieth-century science is a rarity. When he is also a critic of institutional arrange-

ments, aware of omissions and particular strengths of organization in several countries, and may be numbered among the first scientific journalists as well, he becomes an unusual man indeed. J.G. Crowther first became aware of institutional shortcomings in the English technical education establishments in which he taught and sold books from 1919 to 1926. Since then he has travelled widely, visiting countless institutions, many of which made impressions he records, in comments on the German chemical industry, the organization of research in the U.S.S.R., and visits to America. He offers shrewd observations on the popularization of science in expositions and the press, on international scientific cooperation, and on the need for systematic planning of national complexes of research establishments. The reader may be surprised to learn of Lord Rutherford's call for technology assessment in 1936 or the proposal of a code of ethics for science by A.V. Hill, Secretary of the Royal Society, in 1946. Crowther's account of a half century's experiences as an observer of science is replete with topics relevant to present day social concerns — concerns that might today be less pressing if his awareness of the role and consequence of institutions had been more widely shared.

Building the Institutions of Science.
A. Hunter Dupree, *Science in the Federal Government; A History of Policies and Activities to 1940* (205) (Harvard University Press, 1957), x + 460 pp., $7.50.

INTER-RELATIONS OF INSTITUTIONS

Systems Aspects of Changing Institutional Roles.
Philip C. Ritterbush, "Adaptive Response within the Institutional System of Higher Education and Research" (300), *Daedalus,* Summer 70, pp. 648-653.

Design for New Institutional System.
Donald Stotler, *The Self-Learning Society* (301) (Portland, Oregon: Northwest Library Service, Inc., 1970) viii + 153 pp. The author, a science educator who has worked with a wide variety of community organizations in Portland, Oregon, where he presently serves as Science Supervisor for the Public Schools, offers a comprehensive design for the entire system of institutions serving to employ knowledge for social interests. Community centers are recommended for every hundred families, combining the functions of public parks, public schools, youth centers, public libraries, and community centers. Cultural centers will foster interests that require supporting facilities and reference resources. Research centers will extend knowledge, interpret findings for the citizenry, afford apprenticeships for students of all ages, and consult with government. Vocational centers would seek full employment of the talents of their constituents, as well as

help employers to satisfy their needs. Outdoor centers would meet needs for recreation and contemplation. Polity centers would provide forums for policy-making. Cosmological centers would sustain inquiry into meaning and purpose. The author maintains that sweeping institutional realignments are required to create a self-renewing, problem-solving, open society.

The Knowledge Sector.
Fritz Machlup *The Production and Distribution of Knowledge in the United States* (302) (Princeton University Press, 1962), 416 pp., $10.00.

The Institutional System of Knowledge.
Bertram Morris, "Studies in Educational Theory of the John Dewey Society, No. 6," *Institutions of Intelligence* (303) (Ohio State University Press, 1969), viii + 230 pp., $6.00. Reviewed in PROMETHEUS One/two, pp. 14-16.

Institutional Systems and Socioeconomic Functions.
Robert A. Solo, *Economic Organizations and Social Systems* (304) (N.Y.: Bobbs-Merrill, 1967), xiii + 505 pp., $9.75. Recognizes four functional systems performing social functions: market systems, political systems, institutional systems, and familial systems. "Institutional systems organize activities around the commitment of participants to intrinsically valued goals." (p. 360)

Changing System of Research Institutions.
Alvin M. Weinberg, *Reflections on Big Science* (305) (MIT Press, 1967), ix + 182 pp., $6.95, $1.95, paper. New research capabilities have arisen in large multi-purpose laboratories. Weinberg suggests how their missions may be correlated with those of academic institutions.

The Scientific Explosion Transforming Institutions.
Derek J. deSolla Price, *Little Science, Big Science* (306) (Columbia University Press, 1963), xv + 119 pp., $4.50. Argues that the number of scientists and their works has been doubling every fifteen years since 1600, and that one institutional response is the development of "invisible colleges" which circulate preprints and maintain informal communication.

Government Abhors a Policy Vacuum.
Lyman A. Glenny, Robert O. Berdahl, Ernest G. Palola, and James G. Paltridge, *Coordinating Higher Education for the '70s* (307) (Berkeley, Calif.: Center for Research and Development in Higher Education, 1971) xiv, 96 pp. The following are among what the authors regard as minimum powers for state coordinating boards of higher education: "to engage in continuous planning, both long-range and short-range; to acquire information from all postsecondary institutions and agencies through the

establishment of statewide management and data systems; to review and approve new and existing degree programs, new campuses, extension centers, departments and centers of all public institutions, and, where substantial state aid is given, of all private institutions . . ." (p.7) One function proposed in all seriousness for such boards is to analyze the state's needs for manpower while assessing requests to establish new academic programs. If the flow of students across state lines makes this hard to assess, then coordinators may turn to regional higher education boards and interstate compacts. Program review might also extend to major research grants, of (say) $200,000 and up! All of this review effort will of course be based upon comprehensive information systems, such as "the WICHE-PMS systems (which) build on the HEGIS package." (p.77) As "a consequence of better information systems and greater attention to the specific goals of program budgeting and to management-by-objective technologies" such boards may proceed to regulate "the actual outputs of education." (p.78) Freedom is, of course, just another word for nothing left to lose.

Institutional Research Files
John A. Creager and Charles L. Sell, "Research Reports, American Council on Education," *The Institutional Domain of Higher Education, a Characteristics File for Research* (308) , 83 pp. (Nov 69). Details of data collection on institutions of higher education for the research programs of the American Council on Education.

Inter-institutional Dynamics in Research.
Leonard Greenbaum, *A Special Interest; The Atomic Energy Commission, Argonne National Laboratory, and the Midwestern Universities* (309) (University of Michigan Press, 1971) xxii, 222 pp. illus., bibliog. $10.00. Should a national nuclear energy research laboratory be treated as a field facility for the universities of the Midwest or as a national center for which nearby universities serve as a source of visiting students and consulting faculty members? This question received a number of answers as a variety of organizational schemes for the management of the laboratory and its university relationships were tried. Greenbaum brings to the history of institutional relationships a lively curiosity about the concepts guiding them. He describes the play of institutional self interest in an even, sympathetic way, which, however, provokes strong doubt as to the soundness of our present institutional arrangements for research.

Comparison of Institutional Sectors in Research.
Robert S. Merrill, "Some Society-Wide Research and Development Institutions" (311), in National Bureau of Economic Research, *The Rate and Direction of*

Inventive Activity (Princeton University Press, 1962), pp. 409-440. "Pure" academic natural science research, academic medical research, academic engineering research, and government agricultural research are functionally distinct institutional subsystems, each yielding characteristic kinds of studies. "It seems to me that the study of R and D provides both an incentive and an opportunity for broadening still further our knowledge of alternative institutional systems for the performance of social tasks." (p. 434)

Institutional Population Dynamics.
Jonathan A. Gallant and John W. Prothero, "Weight-Watching at the University: The Consequences of Growth" (312), *Science,* 28 Jan 72, pp. 381-88. In an exercise in institutional ecology, two biologists argue that university growth becomes dysfunctional when the student population exceeds 15,000. In 1958, 8 per cent of students in American higher education were enrolled in institutions with total enrollments of more than 20,000. In 1969, the corresponding percentage was 27. "Returning to the natural world, we note again that cells do not grow indefinitely. Instead, they divide." (p. 388)

SOCIAL RELATIONS OF INSTITUTIONS

Stages of Growth and Development of Institutions.
W. J. McGee, "The Relation of Institutions to Environment" (400), *Smithsonian Institution Annual Report for 1895* pp. 701-711. "So organizations which find their germ among the lower organisms attain full development only among enlightened men. At first the organizations are local and reflect the local environment; they grow into institutions, which in like manner reflect the surroundings of the people by whom they are framed; through contact and commingling of peoples the organizations are enlarged and the institutions enriched and made more beneficent; and the institutional laws pass into motives and become the noblest of human characters. In the beginning the organizations, institutions, motives, even, are of the earth earthy, and, like the provincial flora or fauna, pertain to the tract in which they were developed; but through combinations of the good and condemnation of the bad as the organizations spread, they are exalted ever higher and higher in the perfection of humanity. Such is the history of the past, and such the promise for the future." (p. 711).

Systems Aspects of Institutions.
Roderick D. McKenzie, "The Ecology of Institutions" (401) in Amos D. Hawley, ed., *Roderick D. McKenzie on Human Ecology* (University of Chicago Press, 1968), pp. 100-117. In this paper, originally published in 1936, McKenzie defines institution as a unit of collective activity performing a specialized social function. "To comprehend fully the forces involved in institutional location we must take

cognizance of the vital linkages which exist among the diversified units. In other words, we must take the ecological approach." (p. 105)

Institutions Defined.
Everett C. Highes, "The Ecological Aspect of Institutions" (402), *American Sociological Review.* Vol. 1 (1936), pp. 180-92. "There is an order of social phenomena in which the feature of establishment and that of collective behavior meet in a particular way; namely, so that the very form taken by the collective behavior is something socially established. Phenomena of this order are called institutions in this paper." (p. 180) Deals with the influence of spatial contingencies in the interactions and functional specializations of institutions.

The Cultural Mission of Higher Education.
George A. Pettitt, *Prisoners of Culture* (403) (New York: Charles Scribner's Sons, 1970) xii + 292 pp. incl. bibliography, $8.50. A broad anthropological perspective on the interplay of education and preparation for work. Describes many existing arrangements for education as reflecting a "cultural obsession." Considers the role of institutions in cultural change.

Colleges as Open Problem-Solving Networks.
Leonard J. Duhl, "The University and Service to the Community" (404), *EXPERIMENT INNOVATION: New Directions in Education at the University of California,* Vol. 3 (1970), pp. 67-78.

The University as a Social Utility.
Clark Kerr, *The Uses of the University* (405) (Harvard University Press, 1963), vii + 140 pp., $5.00; paper, Harper Torchbooks, $1.60.

Institutionalization of Science.
Joseph Ben-David, "Foundations of Modern Sociology Series," *The Scientist's Role in Society: A Comparative Study* (406) (Englewood Cliffs, N.J.: Prentice-Hall, 1971), xi + 207 pp., $6.95; paper, $2.95. Reviewed in PROMETHEUS One/four by P.C. Ritterbush, pp. 146-47.

A Process Model for Institutional Change.
Lance E. Davis and Douglass C. North, *Institutional Change and American Economic Growth* (407) (Cambridge University Press, 1971) viii, 283 pp. $10.95. Economic studies of institutional structure in finance and manufacturing greatly outnumber studies of institutional dynamics, such as this one, which boldly inquires into the sources of institutional change in the American economy in an attempt to relate the process of growth to its institutional determinants. The definitions offered for the elements of the American economic system are as follows: "(1) The *insti-*

tutional environment is the set of fundamental political, social, and legal ground rules that establishes the basis for production, exchange, and distribution. . . . (2) An *institutional arrangement* is an arrangement between economic units that governs the ways in which these units can cooperate and/or compete. The institutional arrangement is probably the closest counterpart of the most popular use of the term 'institution.' . . . (3) A *primary action group* is a decision-making unit whose decisions govern the process of arrangemental innovation. . . . (4) A *secondary action group* is a decision-making unit that has been established by some change in the institutional arrangement to help effect the capture of income for the primary action group. . . . (5) *Institutional instruments* are documents or devices employed by action groups to effect the capture of income external to the existing arrangemental structures when those instruments are applied within the new arrangemental structure." (pp. 6-9)

> In an attempt to make the reader more familiar with these definitions, consider for a moment the case of a factory that produces smog as well as products. The smoke is part of the production process; it would be costly to eradicate it, but the people living near the factory find it very disagreeable. Assume that the real cost to them of the smoke (as measured by the amount they would be willing to pay to eliminate it) is greater than the cost the factory owner would have to incur if he were to install a smog control device. Clearly total income could be increased if the smog were eliminated; however, it may well be that there is no way the bargain can be effected within the existing institutional arrangement (where the costs of the smoke accrue to one group, the costs of elimination to another). The problem is typical of those faced by residents of almost every city in the United States, and often it appears that some type of government institution should be innovated to effect the smoke abatement. At least two alternatives are open to those who seek the additional income. They could band together to form a political coalition (*a primary action group*), and if successful at the polls, they (or their representatives) could enact a law (*an institutional arrangement*) that prohibited the factory from emitting smoke. Alternatively the successful political coalition could underwrite legislation establishing a zoning board (*secondary action group*), and that board could, in turn, issue a cease and desist order against excessive air pollution. The cease and desist order is an *institutional instrument* backed by the coercive power of the government. (pp. 9-10)

The theory offered in this analysis centers upon four incentives to institutional change: economies of scale, externalities, risk, and transaction costs, which may suffice as motivating factors in most institutional change, whether effected by action groups directly or by manipulating the governmental framework. It is summarized in a diagram which shows four institutional lags that must be overcome to realize profits (an increase in PV = present value) from an improvement in structure. The lags, shown in triangles in the accompanying diagram, are in organization, invention, choice, and start-up.

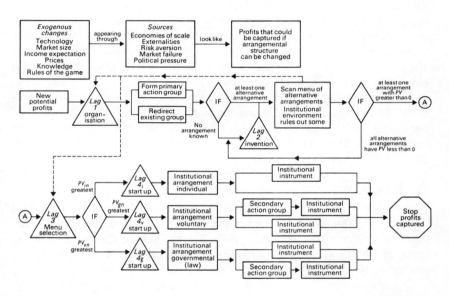

This model appears to be adequate for relating the external environment to the response of institutions, and not just those in the profitmaking sector.

A wedding of economic theory with an explanation of institutional change is essential for further understanding of the process of economic growth — past, present, and future. This is a beginning. Even when the model is not predictive in the sense of providing a single, unique outcome it nevertheless uncovers and makes explicit the forces tending to induce institutional change. It ties together both market and non-market decision making, thus moving in the direction of developing a unified theory of social change. The historical chapters in our view add a whole new dimension to the history of the American economy by permitting us to integrate economic analysis with institutional history in the exploration of the development of product and factor markets. Finally, after three years of developing and applying this model, we are more than ever convinced that this approach does offer a promise of resolving many of the problems discussed . . . and ultimately providing an adequately specified, usefully predictive model of institutional change. (pp. 270-71)

The Poverty of Academicism.
Henry David Aiken, *Predicament of the University* (408) (Indiana University Press, 1971), ix, 404 pp., $11.95. Henry Aiken, Professor of Philosophy at Brandeis, here offers a sensitive and compelling account of the cultural and educational price the modern university has paid for its research preeminence. This book deserves a wide readership in the policy community, especially among those responsible for academic research. His discussion of the distortion of the humanities by supposedly scientific concerns is one of the most satisfying, if saddening, sections of the book. As an account of a life in today's educational and research institutions this book is illuminating and conscientious to a very rare degree. His comments on the narrowness with which rationality is conceived in the university (p. 210) and on their declining intellectual profitability (p. 108) are especially worthy of note.

The Schools Will Not Wither Away.
Herbert Gintis, "Towards a Political Economy of Education: A Radical Critique of Ivan Illich's *Deschooling Society*" (409), *Harvard Educational Review*, Vol. 42, No. 1. (Feb 72), pp. 70-96. Gintis praises the scope of Illich's analysis but disputes his idea that the social function of schools is to nurture consumers. Arguing that their primary function is to produce workers for the lower levels of the production system, he concludes that social restructuring of the schools cannot be painless and will instead entail what Rudi Dutschke has called "the long march through the institutions."

University's Orientation toward Knowledge: Key to Survival.
Robert Nisbet, "The John Dewey Society Lecture — Number Twelve," *The Degradation of the Academic Dogma: The University in America, 1945-1970* (410) (N.Y.: Basic Books, 1971). xviii, 252 pp., $6.95. This sociological essay employs a key distinction between common sense knowledge, of the sort that Descartes imagined Everyman might attain from direct experience, and knowledge based on texts and sources. The latter acquired sanctity during the Middle Ages as a source of religious authority and came to be institutionalized in the university, "distinctly a medieval institution," in the words of one of its most important historians, Hastings Rashdall (*The Universities of Europe in the Middle Ages*, Oxford Uni-

versity Press, 1936, Vol. I, p. 3). Devotion to ritualized learning impresses Nisbet as the central attribute of the university, the core of an academic dogma now greatly eroded by the university's role as a knowledge utility. Society may always secure the knowledge it needs from somewhere — industrial research or study centers — and professionals can be trained in one place or another. But without a strongly shared creed, drawn from some leading function, Nisbet doubts that the university can survive. Shifting his ground from the initial categories of direct knowledge and derived knowledge, he issues a noble-sounding call for an intellectual crusade, based in the university "as a setting for the scholarly and scientific imagination." (p. 207) Its goals are left undefined, as is its relationship to the categories of thought outlined in the opening part of the book. Perhaps the strongest recommendation offered by Professor Nisbet is to secure the future of the university by protecting its lines of communication with its past. He would outlaw the procedure whereby parts of an institution are held to be traditional and therefore to be discarded, or "this is modern and must be lived with no matter how ugly; this is early future and must be built upon." (p. 213) Much institutional planning is naive historicism of this kind. Surely it would be preferable to discover which elements of an institution continue to be fit for its changing circumstances, find out how their adaptive state was achieved and maintained, and then seek to increase their importance within the institution. To sustain the scholarly and scientific imagination could be considered the most important central function for the university, rather than to maintain its own medieval inheritance, but Professor Nisbet leaves the impression that his sympathies lie with the latter. In so doing he undermines his own argument and deprives his final chapter, "The Future of the Academic Community," of much of its force.

Transcending the Complex of Technical Institutions.
Jurgen Habermas, *Toward a Rational Society,* trans. Jeremy Shapiro (411) (Boston: Beacon Press, 1970), 127 pp., $5.95. Reviewed by Phillip Scribner in PROMETHEUS One/five, pp. 65-73.

Humane Reason Seeks a New Social Context.
Jurgen Habermas, *Knowledge and Human Interests,* trans. Jeremy Shapiro (412) (Boston: Beacon Press, 1971), 356 pp., $7.50. Reviewed by Phillip Scribner in PROMETHEUS One/five, pp. 65-73.

The Social Context of Higher Education.
President's Commission on Campus Unrest, "The Scranton Report" (413), *The Chronicle of Higher Education,* Vol. 5, no. 2 (5 Oct 70), 24 pp.

Scientific Autonomy and Institutional Equilibrium.
Don K. Price, *The Scientific Estate* (414) (Harvard University Press, 1965), xi +
323 pp. Considers the practical relations of scientific institutions to the economy
and the government, the theoretical relationship of science to practical values,
and to the principles underlying the constitutional system.

APPRAISALS OF INSTITUTIONS

Major Advances from Major Institutions.
Karl W. Deutsch, John Platt, and Dieter Senghaas, "Conditions Favoring Major
Advances in Social Science; Analysis of 62 Advances Since 1900 Shows that Most
Came from a Few Centers and Have Rapid Effects" (500), *Science,* Vol. 171 (5 Feb
71), pp. 450-59. Credits major intellectual centers affording scope to interdisciplinary research with nearly one-half of major social science advances from 1900-
1929 and two-thirds thereafter.

University Governance in Process of Change.
David D. Dill, *Case Studies in University Governance* (501) (Washington, D.C.:
National Association of State Universities and Land-Grant Colleges, 1971) 154
pp. + appendices, $3.00. Case studies of new governance structures at Florida
A&M University, the University of Minnesota, Columbia University, and the
University of New Hampshire, each of which had had at least one year's experience
with its new structure at the time of the study. In each case the author provides a
chronology of events leading to the creation of each structure, with emphasis on
the planning process. He focuses on selected aspects of each system in operation
and includes proposed or completed changes in the applied system. In the section
entitled "Implications of the Case Studies," the author remarks on the surprising
frequency with which administrators, students, and faculty members "posed a
parliamentary model of decision making. . . .The desire for such a model seems
to further emphasize that the contemporary American university, like its parent
society, is confused as to what its goals should be, and that this confusion necessarily leads to an emphasis on political process. The support for a parliamentary
model seemed to exude from the hope that a president would appear with a new
raison d'etre for the university and would lead the academic community out of its
wilderness."

Bleakness of the Schools.
Charles E. Silberman, *Crisis in the Classroom: The Remaking of American Education* (502) (New York: Random House, 1970) 525 pp., $10.00. This book was
written "to discuss, in concrete detail, the ways in which schools, colleges, and
mass media educate: not only *what* they teach, but *how* they teach, and in particular the manifold and frequently unconscious ways in which how they teach

determines what it is that people actually learn. This is, in addition, a book about how the schools should be improved, about how they *can* be improved, the case for change being argued in the main through descriptions of schools in operation now; and it is a book about how colleges and universities might help bring these changes about by educating new kinds of educators and by developing the knowledge on which their performance might be based." Mr. Silberman argues that public schools are grim, joyless, oppressive, intellectually sterile, esthetically barren, that teachers and principals lack civility and unconsciously display contempt for children as children. He maintains, however, that this system can be changed because the wrongs are "due not to venality or indifference or stupidity, but to mindlessness. . . . This mindlessness—the failure or refusal to think seriously about educational purpose, the reluctance to question established practice—is not the monopoly of the public school; it is diffused remarkably evenly throughout the entire educational system, and indeed the entire society." The solution to this problem must lie in "infusing the various educating institutions with purpose, . . .with thought about purpose, and about the ways in which techniques, content, and organization fulfill or alter purpose." Institutions must continuously engage in self-examination. Educators must be taught the importance of defining institutional goals and of changing goals when necessary.

Institutions as Magic Theaters of Temperament.
Martin Green, *Cities of Light and Sons of the Morning; A Cultural Psychology for an Age of Revolution* (503) (Boston: Little, Brown and Co., 1972), xi + 456 pp., illus., index, $15.00. Reviewed by P.C. Ritterbush in PROMETHEUS One/five, pp. 81-83.

Institutional Change— A Variable That Eludes Measurement.
Harold Hodgkinson, Carnegie Commission on Higher Education, 1947 Center Street, Berkeley, Calif. 94704, *Institutions in Transition; A Study of Change in Higher Education* (504), v + 169 pp., $6.00. The changes most apparent from analysis of U.S. Office of Education statistics, on which this study is based, are of much less consequence than challenges to the social and economic allegiances of institutions of higher education and the programmatic and structural contradictions revealed by qualitative analysis. The author notes with some surprise that such data reveal no consistent patterns of difference among institutions— that the diversity for which the system is so often praised cannot be discovered in statistical summaries. A questionnaire was employed to elicit responses about change from college and university presidents. Again, the results are unenlightening, largely because the variables that are usually measured by the institutions contribute so little to assessing performance. The percentage of students continuing on to graduate and professional school may be an index of the academic strength of an undergraduate program and the motivation of students enrolled, but it cannot be considered a measure of institutional "effectiveness." Nor can

the "openness" of an institution be gauged from the heterogeneity of its student body alone. This concept requires an appraisal of an institution's responsiveness to social interests. Quantitative indicators, especially when based on the data normally available in our institutions, are seriously inadequate in dealing with concepts such as institutional effectiveness and openness. What is one to make of a category designated "institutional purpose" in which 1043 institutions are classified as "multi-purpose" and 138 as "single purpose"? Is every change in any measurable variable to be considered an "institutional change" just because it takes place within an institution or should that term imply fundamental change of purpose, priorities, or primary allegiances? If it is the latter there is as yet no generally agreed way to measure it and there will continue to be wide disagreement as to how much significant change has occurred, how much ought to take place, and how much the system can stand. Perhaps the central question of higher education policy today, it remains unanswered.

INSTITUTIONAL CHANGE AND ALTERNATIVE INSTITUTIONS

Anthology on New Directions.
Robert Buckhout and 81 Concerned Berkeley Students, *Toward Social Change; A Handbook for Those Who Will* (600) (N.Y.: Harper & Row, 1971) xiii + 480 pp., $6.95 paper. Collection of articles, excerpts, and commentary on the following themes: the possibility and desirability of social change, "Naderism" in the social sciences, the third world experience, violence, alienation, alternate life styles, the drug scene, encounter groups, mental health, population control, and educational reform. Includes bibliography.

Strategies for Change Are Needed.
Frederick de W. Bolman, "Problems of Change and Changing Problems" (601), *Journal of Higher Education,* Vol. 41 (1970), pp. 589-598. In this excellent short article the Executive Director of the Esso Education Foundation calls for understanding of three ingredients of institutional change: a conceptual understanding of how guided change takes place, an awareness of the status of change as applied knowledge, and the ability to recognize its institutional prerequisites. "I believe that broad-gauged humanists, social scientists, and scientists should collaborate constantly to redefine and restructure our colleges and universities in the light of new developments in the learning process." (p. 590)

Failings of Higher Education Inherent in the Institutional System.
Committee on Higher Education, Office of the Secretary, Department of Health, Education, and Welfare. *Report on Higher Education* (602). U.S. Government Printing Office, 1971 (HE 5.250: 50065), $1.00. A devastating broad-front criticism of the institutional failings of higher education, which occasioned a strong

sense of injury among the staffs of Washington-based education associations. A logical sequel to the report would be an analysis of all the changes required in the U.S. Office of Education and other government agencies in order to make it possible to implement its recommendations.

Alternative Institutions in Higher Education.

Everett Reimer, *An Essay on Alternatives in Education* (603) (30 June 70), 94 pp. Published by the Centro Intercultural de Documentacion (CIDOC), Apartado 479, Cuernavaca, Mexico.

Condemnation of Institutional System of Schools.

Ivan Illich, *Deschooling Society* (604) (New York: Harper & Row, 1971) 160 pp., $6.00. This bold call for the disestablishment of the state religion of public education raises a host of questions about the social effects of schools. Illich is adamantly opposed to meritocracy and champions literacy for all by dismantling the schools that presently function more as a progressive series of filters than as channels of opportunity. It might be argued that "real learning" has never been confined to schools. If elite roles in the society will no longer be as circumscribed as they have been, there is no other genuine need for an exclusionary system of the sort that schools have for so long been. Without changes in the structure of our communities it seems unlikely that the "free school movement" will succeed in converting the massive bureaucratized complex of schools to more humane settings for learning. They seem to face a certain prospect of irreversible decline.

Institutions Can Be Changed.

Garth N. Jones, *Planned Organizational Change; A Study in Change Dynamics* (605) (N.Y. and Washington, D.C.: Frederick A. Praeger, 1969) xxiv + 243 pp., incl. bibliog., $6.50. Reviewed in PROMETHEUS One/two, pp. 16-18.

Creating a Sense of Community.

Warren Bryan Martin, *Alternative to Irrelevance: A Strategy for Reform in Higher Education* (606) (Nashville: Abingdon Press, 1968) 156 pp. $1.95 paper. Educational institutions must be open now to creative alternatives because our present institutions have little "transfer value" for the next century of what will probably be an entirely different kind of learning, in both form and content. The author states a strong case for the definition of institutional goals by *all* members of a given college community. For large institutions, a sense of community is possible in "cluster colleges". The cluster college concept is also the best mechanism we now have for testing divergent educational models within the institutional system.

Program for College Reform.

Harold Taylor, *How to Change Colleges: Notes on Radical Reform* (607) (New York: Holt, Rinehart and Winston, 1971) 180 pp. $4.95. Also in paper. "The (student) revolt. . .had a deeply educational effect in redefining the mission of the university" and defining its responsibility for political, social, and moral action. Harold Taylor questions "whether the universities have finally accepted responsibility for taking the students seriously, and whether they are now prepared to serve as centers of creative thought and action for meeting the problems of the students and their society." If not, "they should move over and give the students a chance to invent their own university. Some of the students are already trying to do that, and they need help. This book is about how to give it to them." The author, a well-known champion of educational reform, wrote this book as a successor to *Students Without Teachers* (New York: McGraw Hill, 1969) xiv + 321 pp. $7.95.

POLICY, PLANNING, AND INSTITUTIONAL OBJECTIVES

Objectives of Institutions of Higher Education.
Richard E. Peterson, "The Crisis of Purpose: Definition and Uses of Institutional Goals" (700), Oct 70, 13 pp. + bibliography. Report 5, ERIC Clearinghouse on Higher Education, 1 Dupont Circle, NW, Room 630, Washington, D.C. 20036.

Controversy over Political Discussions in the Lab.
Philip M. Boffey, "Science and Politics: Free Speech Controversy at Lawrence Laboratory" (701), *Science,* Vol. 169 (21 Aug 70) pp. 743-45. Deals with attempts by the laboratory management to define limits to staff participation in political discussions during working hours.

Association for Institutional Research.
Proceedings of annual forums on institutional research in higher education. (702)

Institutional Management Systems.
Charles B. Johnson and William G. Katzenmeyer, *Management Information Systems in Higher Education: The State of the Art* (703) (Duke University Press, 1969) xi + 191 pp. Proceedings of a seminar held at Duke University, June 1969. The lead essay, by George Baughman of Ohio State University, and his comments on the national "Higher Education General Information Survey" of the U.S. Office of Education, deal with procedures for the study of institutional systems and exemplify the applicability of historical and social science research findings to institutional management.

The Search for Identifiable Outputs of Higher Education.
Western Interstate Commission on Higher Education, *The Outputs of Higher Education:Their Identification, Measurement, and Evaluation* (704) (July 70) vii, 130 pp. $3.50. Seminar papers and bibliography, available from WICHE, P.O. Drawer P, Boulder, Colo. 80302.

Budgetary Chaos and Statewide Coordination.
Frederick Betz and Carlos Kruytbosch, "Sponsored Research and University Budgets: A Case Study in American University Government" (705) , *Minerva,* Vol.7 (1970), pp.492-519. A case study of the University of California that demonstrates how institutional integrity can be lost in conflicts of purpose and procedure in the support of research.

Institutional Objectives and Competent Action.
George S. Odiorne, *Management Decision by Objectives* (706) (Englewood Cliffs, N.J.: Prentice-Hall, 1969), $8.95. Reviewed by P.C. Ritterbush in PROMETHEUS One/three, pp. 65-69.

Objectives of Bureaucratic Organizations.
Henry L. Tosi, John R. Rizzo, and Stephen J. Carroll, "Setting Goals in Management by Objectives" (707), *California Management Review,* Vol. 12, no. 4 (Summer 70), pp. 70-78.

Self-Realization of Institution Members—A Major Objective.
Harry Levinson, "Management by Whose Objectives?" (708), *Harvard Business Review,* Vol. 48, no. 4 (July-Aug 70), pp. 125-134.

Funding Patterns and Institutional Incoherence.
Frederick Betz, Carlos Kruytbosch, and David Stimson, "Funds, Fragmentation, and the Separation of Functions in the State University" (709), *Social Science Information,* Vol. 8, No. 1 (1970), pp. 131-148.

Goal Identification.
Norman P. Uhl, "Research Monograph Number Two" *Identifying Institutional Goals* (710) National Laboratory for Higher Education, Durham, North Carolina (1971), iii + 86 pp.

Goals Survey of American Universities.
E.W. Gross and P.V. Grambsch, *University Goals and Academic Power* (711) (Washington, D.C.: American Council on Education, 1968) $3.50. 164 pp.

Outputs of Higher Education.
Ian McNett, "Assessing College Effectiveness" (712) , *Change* (Jan.-Feb., 1971), pp.13-14. Report on the status of the Planning and Management Systems program of the Western Interstate Conference on Higher Education (WICHE), and its attempt to evolve "output indicators" for higher education.

Failure of Collegial Policy-Making.
Dwight R. Ladd, *Change in Educational Policy: Self-Studies in Selected Colleges and Universities* (713) (N.Y.: McGraw Hill, 1970). 231 pp. $5.95. For the Carnegie Commission on Higher Education. Analysis of thirteen attempts to reformulate educational policy by consultation and consensus, conducted in the 1960s at leading institutions, led Ladd to conclude that "we have passed the limits of collegiality as an effective system of decision-making." He also described faculty resistance to recommendations for change.

Decision-Making in the University.
Dwight R. Ladd. Paper for the National Conference on Higher Education, March, 1971. 13 pp. (714) If all constituencies of an institution were well represented on its board, they could grant its president much more effective power than usual, and enforce accountability by oversight and review.

Evaluation of Foundation Activities.
Stephen White. N.Y.: Alfred P. Sloan Foundation, 1970. Occasional Paper, 15 pp. (715) On request, 630 Fifth Avenue, New York, N.Y. 10020.

Academic Policy and Institutional Integrity.
Stephen J. Tonsor, "Power, Authority, and University Administration" (716) , *Congressional Record,* 27 Oct 71, S16883-87. Proposes that policy-making authority be vested in university boards of trustees, aided by an investigative secretariat, and criticizes faculties for selfish attention to their personal and professional interests at the expense of institutional integrity. Entered into the *Congressional Record* by Senator James Buckley (R., N.Y.).

Society for College and University Planning.
Publishes a bimonthly bulletin, *News,* with occasional inserts of essays and articles. Annual subscription $10.00 in North America, $15.00 elsewhere. Proceedings of three annual conferences on campus planning available: 1966 ($2.00), 1967 ($5.00), and 1968 ($4.00); also *An Annotated Bibliography on University Planning and Development* (1969), 158 pp., $5.00 and *Campus-Community Relationships, An Annotated Bibliography* (April 71), 63 pp., devoted to geographical topics. H. Gilbert Nicol, Director, 616 West 114th Street, New York, N.Y. 10025. (717)

Institutional Research in the University: A Handbook

By Paul Dressel and associates. (718) (San Francisco: Jossey-Bass, 1971) $12.50. Large universities generally establish offices of institutional research to achieve uniformity in statistics on enrollment. The functions of such offices have been broadened to include the collection of many different kinds of data, which makes them centers for statistics on institutional activities. This handbook offers a reinterpretation of institutional research as the evaluative self-study of a college's goals, operations, and accomplishments. It advances proposals for the establishment, organization, and operation of offices of institutional research in academic institutions, on the assumption that statistical data have ready applicability to the determination of policies.

Institutional Research, Early Development.

A. J. Brumbaugh, *Research Designed to Improve Institutions of Higher Learning* (719) (Washington: American Council on Education, 1960) 56 pp. E.D.R.S. 017-141 $0.25 MF, $2.32 H.C. This important study helped to lay a foundation for expanded programs of institutional research oriented toward the policy needs of institutions of higher education. The examples given and the arguments advanced tend to indicate that the early contributions of institutional research were to functional efficiency rather than instrumental service to distinctive institutional objectives.

Institutional Research, Lack of Academic Impact.

Ernest L. Boyer, *Institutional Research and the Academic Program* (720), "New Dimensions in Higher Education" No.20 (U.S. Department of Health, Education, and Welfare, U.S. Office of Education, April 67), 76 pp. E.D.R.S. 013-381 $0.50 MF, $3.04 HC. Boyer cited three major areas of institutional research which had constructively influenced institutional management: facilities studies, cost-analyses, and enrollment studies. But he found no comparable contributions to academic program: "the curricular and instructional dimensions of higher education have remained relatively fixed." (p.20) He entered six recommendations aimed at enhancing the policy applicability of institutional research:
1. to sharpen the identity and purposes of institutional research as a profession,
2. to probe more fundamental educational problems.
3. to develop comprehensive and empirically supported theories,
4. to orient institutional research toward institutional change,
5. to disseminate findings more effectively, and
6. to become part of an institution's commitment to change.

"The immensely important activity of institutional research has failed, on the whole, to make significant contributions to the real business of education, which is to do the best possible job of transmitting knowledge, stimulating the growth of intellectual maturity, and discovering new knowledge. . . . What is in short supply is the wholehearted desire to seek better ways to teach, to communicate, to administer. If nature abhors a vacuum, it also resists displacement; and human nature, having had several thousand years to refine natural law, tends to resist forces that even seem to lead toward personal displacement. And so when all is said and done, the question of whether educational research is to become a vital force in academic affairs depends on the individual faculty member, dean, department head, president, addressing his own professional posture and saying, 'There may be a better way . . .' and meaning it." (pp.46-47)

Attempt to Measure Institutional Goals.
Educational Testing Service, *Institutional Goals Inventory* (721) (Princeton, N.J.: Educational Testing Service, 1971) 13 pp. The number of institutional goal areas has been expanded to 22, with some amendment of the 18 originally tested by Norman Uhl. The list of goals statements has been expanded to 110. The instrument was tested at ten institutions in California in May in hopes of issuing a revised version for more general use in the fall of 1971. For a narrative account of the development of the revised instrument see Richard E. Peterson, "Toward Institutional Goal-Consciousness" (722) (Berkeley, Calif.: Educational Testing Service, June 71). The following outputs are recognized in this version:
1. academic development (acquisition of knowledge, academic mastery, etc.),
2. intellectual orientation (as an attitude, style, commitment to learning, etc.),
3. individual personal development (of one's unique human potential, etc.),
4. humanism/altruism (idealism, social concern, etc.),
5. cultural/esthetic awareness (appreciation, sensitivity to the arts, etc.),
6. traditional religiousness,
7. vocational preparation,
8. advanced training (graduate, professional),
9. research,
10. meeting local needs (community public service, etc.),
11. public service (to regional, state, national, international agencies),
12. social egalitarianism (meeting educational needs of people throughout the social system),
13. social criticism/activism (toward change in American life).
    All of the above are considered to be output goals and those that

follow, support goals:

14. freedom (academic, personal),
15. democratic governance (emphasizing structural factors),
16. community (emphasizing attitudinal factors—morale, spirit, ethos),
17. intellectual/esthetic environment (intellectual stimulation, excitement, etc.),
18. collegiate environment (extracurricular activities, social life, athletics, etc.),
19. innovation,
20. evaluation and planning,
21. accountability/efficiency, and
22. external relations (toward understanding and mutually beneficial relations between campus and external constituencies).

Facilities Planning and Innovation.
Educational Facilities Laboratory, 477 Madison Avenue, New York, New York 10022. *College Newsletter* (723), occasional publication on studies of physical facilities being pursued by EFL. The current issue, number ten (24 pp.) features experimental light construction techniques employing thin membranes, now being planned for Antioch (Columbia, Md.), La Verne College (San Diego, Calif.) and Princeton University.

Institutional Settings for Research.
Frederick Betz, "On the Management of Inquiry" (724), *Management Science,* Vol. 18, no. 4, part 1 (Dec 71), pp. B117-133. Suggests that professional roles and styles of inquiry may be correlated with different kinds of institutional settings.

Vigorous Call for Institutional Self-Awareness.
American Academy of Arts and Sciences, *A First Report: The Assembly on University Goals and Governance* (725) Available from the Assembly at 7 Linden Street, Cambridge, Mass. 02138. This first report of the Assembly presents 85 theses related to the goals and internal organization of colleges and universities, formulated as policy propositions for discussion and testing. The theses grow out of nine basic themes which are carried through the entire set of theses. One theme is "Knowledge as a Basis for Educational Reform: To improve and reform higher education—not to calm dissidents but to achieve the potentialities of colleges and universities—a kind of knowledge is required that does almost everything—the natural environment, government and industry, all manner of other institutions foreign and domestic—but they are loathe to scrutinize themselves and the institutions they inhabit. If reform is not to be mindless, knowledge and data are needed on the character and effects of present educational and research programs.

It is essential to know more about how decisions are made and executed in colleges and universities, and how the successes and failures of innovations are communicated so that others may learn from the experiences of those who have experimented with new approaches. Institutional self-study is desirable; it does not suffice for presidents and administrative staff to be interested in such matters. The methods, content, and philosophy of education need to become a more vital interest of many professors, staff and students." Other important themes are: 1) Institutions of higher education must reassert *learning* as their central mission; 2) Higher education should be a "considered choice" rather than an unavoidable prescription for young people, so it is the obligation of all institutions of higher education to clearly define their particular educational strengths and admissions criteria and to convince employers that college attendance is not the only way to certify employment capabilities; 3) The diversity of higher education must be preserved and extended, therefore we must learn to appreciate and understand institutional differences and not pattern every school on the same model; and 4) Strong executive leadership is essential for every university, exercised with consideration given to the opinions and values of the whole university community, and accountable to that community. The theses which follow from these themes have been soundly thought out and deserve consideration. They clearly reflect an appreciation of the existing system but emphasize at the same time that "much of what exists is of recent origin and can be altered." Alteration and reform require serious self-study, planning, and articulation of goals, and the Assembly stresses the need for all of these.

Governance: a Little Understood Institutional Process.

Harold L. Hodgkinson, *Campus Governance: The Amazing Thing Is That It Works at All* (726), Report 11, ERIC Clearinghouse on Higher Education, One Dupont Circle, N.W., Washington, D.C. 20036, 22 pp., incl. bibliography of 291 items covering the period 1965-70, classified as Research-based material on governance; Trustees: theory, opinion and research; The President and other administrators: theory, research, and opinion; Research on faculty and governance; Statements of opinion on faculty and governance; Research on student protest having implications for governance; Policy recommendations on student participation; General articles on student participation in governance; Legal and political dimensions of governance; Major policy statements on campus governance; Compendia; Typical institutional governance statements; and General works on campus governance. The author complains that governance is little understood, and proposes avenues of research, but fails to consider the possibility that governance must founder in contradiction unless institutions define their objectives.

HUMAN VALUES WITHIN INSTITUTIONS

Toward a Transformation of Technical Civilization.
Theodore Roszak, *The Making of a Counter Culture; Reflections on the Technocratic Society and Its Youthful Opposition* (800) (Garden City, N.Y.: Doubleday Anchor Books, 1969), xiv + 303 pp., $1.95.

The Unconscious Evils of Organization and Technology.
Charles A. Reich, "The Limits of Duty" (801) , *The New Yorker,* 19 June 71, pp. 52-57. "Law should be based on the assumption that institutions, more than individuals, are likely to go astray. Perhaps the primary regulatory work of law should be shifted from that of managing people to that of managing organizations while safeguarding the individuality of the people within them."

Digest of Youth Conference Recommendations.
Wade Green, *Youth's Agenda for the Seventies; A Report on the White House Conference on Youth with a Summary of the Recommendations* (802) (New York: The JDR 3rd Fund, 1971) 96 pp., distribution limited, may be reissued. Following Wade's valuable introduction, this report summarizes the recommendations of the Conference in brief compass— a compact guide which may usefully be read with a companion volume issued by the Fund, *The Changing Values on Campus* (811) (N.Y.: Pocket Books, 1972).

Institutional Responsiveness to Youth.
White House Conference on Children and Youth, *Federal Executive Branch Review of the Recommendations of the 1971 White House Conference on Youth* (802) (U.S. Government Printing Office, 1972, O-454-949), 414 pp., $3.75. To the Conference indictment of the inadequacy of career counseling, the Department of Labor responds that federal support for that function is vested in the Department of Health, Education, and Welfare and that its own Employment Service primarily serves those who are out of school. While the recommended Department of Human Resources would consolidate these efforts, "We are now exploring ways to improve the quality and quantity of job information and predictions available to students and way to introduce it the schools. . . ." (p. 246) The recommendation that a national job information service be established was accepted by the Labor Department "as a long range goal." Interim measures include daily computer-generated listings of vacancies entered with the Employment Service and their gradual extension statewide, now being tested in four states. The Department's reply to the recommendation favoring the humanization of work was that their Employment Standards Division has started triennial national surveys of job

satisfaction and will undertake an inventory of employer motivations. The compilation of such an extensive series of responses to youth concerns by government agencies is unprecedented and worthwhile, yet the document is more revealing than encouraging. Government agencies are so dedicated to merchandising their programs that they resist reappraisals, especially those tending to favor alternatives under the jurisdiction of a competing agency. Stolid offical responses of course mask the human qualities that distinguish the staff of many agencies, but the patterns of thought they disclose are governing realities. The contrast between the recommendations as set out in the *Report of the White House Conference on Youth* (1971, 310 pp., $2.50) and the response of agencies deserves attention and careful analysis.

Inglorious Institutions and Radical Sentiments.

Bennett M. Berger, reviews of four recent books on communes (803) , *The New York Times Book Review* (14 Nov 71), p. 6ff. Berger thinks the establishment of anti-technological communes results in part from "the failure of American mainstream rhetoric to ennoble technological civilization. It is remarkable and shocking suddenly to realize that we live in a society that has somehow neglected to sanctify, in a way that intelligent and sophisticated people can affirm, the institutions we have created and the kinds of persons those institutions constrain us to become. Our society is bureaucratic from top to bottom, but nobody praises bureaucracy. . . . A culture that cannot convincingly celebrate the goals and the types of human character it is in fact dedicated to producing must expect to lose some of the best of its young and some of its elders who have discovered that they can do without rewards that sour when there are no convictions to keep them fresh." (p. 32)

Toward a More Humane Idea of Civic Leadership.

Ren Frutkin, "Success: Who Needs It?" (804), *Yale Alumni Magazine*, June 71, pp. 6-11.

Institutional Identity and Professional Values.

Burton R. Clark, *The Distinctive College: Antioch, Reed & Swarthmore* (805) (Chicago: Aldine Publishing Co., 1970), vi + 280 pp., $8.95. Holds that the distinctiveness of these colleges, upon which their success depends, has been achieved through the development of an "institutional saga." "It offers in the present a particular definition of the organization as a whole and suggests common characteristics of members. Its definitions are deeply internalized by many members, thereby becoming a part, even an unconscious part, of individual motive. A saga is, then, a mission made total across a system in space and time. It embraces the participants of a given day and links together successive waves of participants over major periods of time." (p. 235) See also his "Belief and Loyalty in College

Organization," *Journal of Higher Education,* Vol. 42 (1971), pp. 499-515 or "The Organizational Saga in Higher Education," *Administrative Science Quarterly,* June 72, pp. 178-184.

Commitment Taking Its Course.

Michael Rossman, *The Wedding within the War* (806)) (N.Y.: Doubleday Anchor Books, 1971), vi + 397 pp. Rossman came to Berkeley as a student in 1958, when the earliest intimations of the enterprise that has become the new left were stirring. He describes the arousal of political emotions in the protest vigil at the Chessman execution and the protest against the House UnAmerican Activities Committee, both in 1960, and recounts his experience of the Free Speech Movement at Berkeley in 1964 as the emergence of a sensibility that fed on shared decision and the generation of values by action. "It signalled the Tearing Loose—the active beginning of the end of my life within the old institutions. . ." (p. 92) A collection of articles covering ten years of arousal and estrangement that makes a first-rate political autobiography.

Faculty Attitudes and Institutional Culture.

Charles B. Spaulding and Henry A. Turner, "Political Orientation and Field of Specialization among College Professors" (807), *Sociology of Education,* Vol. 18 (1968), pp. 247-262.

Radical Activism—A Force in Institutions

The Archives of Institutional Change is collecting reports and documents on radical activism in institutions of learning; contributions are solicited. (808)

Thoughts on Bureaucracy.

Erich Fromm, "Free for All" (809)\, *Management Science,* Vol. 16 (1970), B-699-705. Editorial on the need for humanist methods for the management of human enterprise.

Cultural Contradictions Affecting the Knowledge Sector

Kenneth Keniston, *Youth and Dissent; The Rise of a New Opposition* (810) (N.Y.: Harcourt Brace Jovanovich, 1971), xii + 403 pp., paper, $2.95. These collected essays are the harvest of ten years' writing by the Yale psychologist who has become one of the most perceptive observers of contemporary youth. He leaves little room for the view that dissident acts reflect a calculated destructive program, arguing instead that contradiction between the critical perception of better-educated young people and the situations they experience drive them to restless antagonism. The university functions as "the protest-promoting institution" as a result of "the gap between student hopes and institutional facts." (p. 158) He finds little to support Lewis Fewer, Daniel Bell, or Zbigniew Brezinski in their view of young radicals as counterrevolutionaries against the imminent triumph of large-scale organization and electronic communications. Wide-scale dissent among the privileged young challenges a whole cluster of theories which presupposed the continuing stability of western democracies. "The emergence of a youthful opposition, then, demands new theories not only of youthfulness but of human nature, of society, and of their relationship." (p. 375)

Willingness of Youth to Work in Mainstream Institutions.

JDR 3rd Fund, *Youth and the Establishment; A Report on Research for John D. Rockefeller 3rd and the Task Force on Youth by Daniel Yankelovich, Inc.* (812) (New York, JDR 3rd Fund, Inc., 1971), 89 pp. Single copies on request from the JDR 3rd Fund, Inc., 59 Rockefeller Plaza, New York, New York 10020. Youth cooperation with community, business, and government leaders, an appraisal of mutual interest, for a Task Force on Youth formed by John D. Rockefeller 3rd, based on a national survey by Daniel Yankelovich, Inc. The report's 36 findings may be summarized as follows:

There is broad agreement among students and establishment leaders on many of the most pressing areas of domestic social need that warrant attention— poverty, race relations, pollution, reform of the political process, and the legal system;

Beneath their anger, establishment leaders are keenly interested in working with the students, sympathetic to their goals and even their feelings;

Beneath their mistrust of the establishment, the majority of students want to work with establishment leaders;

The majority of the media to the contrary, the overwhelming majority of the student body is moderate, antiviolent, and desirous of working within the system; and

Millions of students, especially the forerunner group, are ready to devote time and effort, at minimal compensation and at the cost of postponing their individual career paths, to working toward the solution of pressing social problems (pp. 85-86).

MANAGEMENT, ADMINISTRATION, ORGANIZATIONAL BEHAVIOR

Appraisal of Status of the Field of Organizational Behavior.

Dwight Waldo, Martin Landau, Hans H. Jecht, Glenn D. Paige, "The Study of Organizational Behavior: Status, Problems, and Trends" (900), 58 pp. No. 8 of Special Series, "Papers in Comparative Public Administration" sponsored by the Comparative Administration Group of the American Society for Public Administration. Available from the Society, 1225 Connecticut Avenue, N.W., Washington, D.C. 20036.

Organizational Change.

John Platt "Hierarchical Restructuring; Sudden Jumps to New Levels of Organization Occur in Personality Changes and Social Revolutions Like the Present" (901) (May 70), 27 pp. Communication 269, Mental Health Research Institute, University of Michigan.

Case Study of Institutional Change.
Sherman K. Grinnell, "The Informal Action Group: One Way to Collaborate in a University" (902), *The Journal of Applied Behavioral Science,* Vol. 5, No. 1 (1969) pp. 74-109. One in a series of "Case Studies of Behavioral Science Interaction."

Institutional Appraisal and the Search for Leadership.
Frederick deW. Bolman, *How College Presidents Are Chosen* (903) (Washington, D.C.:American Council on Education, 1965), 60 pp. $1.00. Of 115 new college presidents surveyed, 48 reported no specific or detailed discussion in advance of their appointment about the formal long-range plans of the institutions over which they had been chosen to preside. Bolman strongly recommends that the search for leadership begin with a sophisticated determination of the needs of the institution, quoting one faculty member of a selection committee as follows: "The board of trustees and any selection committee should make a thorough analysis of an institution, and of the immediate goals of that institution, before undertaking to hunt for a president. I think few institutions really take the task seriously; certainly this institution didn't. But it is idiotic to build lists of names or to enumerate criteria for a president if you don't know where your institution stands, where it wants to go, and what it needs in the way of an executive head." (pp.23-24)

Activity Measures for the Single Institution.
Educational Testing Service, *Institutional Functioning Inventory* (904)[(Princeton, N.J.: Educational Testing Service, 1970). Available from the Institutional Research Program for Higher Education, Eldon Park, Director. A survey instrument with 72 questions for students and 60 additional questions for faculty, administrators, and others, whereby they may indicate attitudes and awareness of institutional characteristics and programs, is now offered to institutions of higher education by the Educational Testing Service. Also available, "Prospectus" 18 pp. and "Preliminary Technical Manual" vi, 63 pp.

Origins of Institutional Functioning Inventory.
Educational Testing Service, *Conversations toward a Definition of Institutional Vitality; Background Discussions during the Development of a Measure of Vitality in American Colleges and Universities* (905) (Princeton: Educational Testing Service, 1967, 112, xiii pp. Conference transcripts of discussions about problems of measuring the vitality of educational institutions.

Human Factors in the Change Process.
Raymond G. Studer, "Human Systems Design and the Management of Change" (906), *General Systems,* Vol. 16 (1971), pp. 131-143. Human system designs may be cast so as to serve as goals for directive processes of change. In order to do so, both the environment for such systems and the

pattern of desired activity or behavior must be specified, even though their interactions cannot be predicted in detail. Studer offers this caveat:

"Even in its generality this has been a rather laborious approach to dealing with the future. A straightforward forecast or description of a desirable future would have perhaps been much simpler. But one must take seriously Karl Popper's warning (in *The Open Society and Its Enemies,* Princeton University Press, 1962) that we should not commit ourselves to a particular plan for the future. Quite aside from our inability to predict the events which will alter such plans, overcommitment to the ideologies which inevitably accompany them has led to human disasters which we do not want to repeat. I favor, along with many others, a flexible but controlled approach to the future, where any number of plans are realizable. Uncertainty is, and probably will remain, a fundamental condition of man, but uncertainty obviously does not preclude action. It is perhaps true that there is no progress — only process — in human affairs, and there are probably no solutions to human problems, per se. Our ability to respond incisively to human dysfunctions is, within the bounds of present knowledge, critically limited. More important, human problems change before solutions to them can be realized. In approaching the future, our design objective should respond more directly to the variable nature of open, living systems. . . . A planning committed to adjustment and change is one in which the process of living becomes a process of systematic experimentation to upgrade human existence." (p. 140)

Managing Change within Research Organizations.
Evelyn Glatt and Maynard W. Shelly, *The Research Society* (907) (New York: Gordon and Breach, 1968) xiv + 549 pp., .$28.00. A collection of twenty-two papers on problems of management and organization in research establishments, in memory of Raymond Hainer of Arthur D. Little, Inc. While there is much in this collection that illuminates the internal functioning of research establishments and management attitudes, relatively little is to be found about the directions for future change which have become a topic of anxious debate within them. In a penetrating epilogue Donald Schon dwells on the inadequacies of managerial procedures in dealing with problems which arise from the transformation of the very disciplines within which such establishments work. Rather than seek an ideal organizational model, laboratory managers should anticipate an existential quest for identity, an anguished confrontation with uncertainty. Organizations that fail to provide for soul-searching about their objectives would be like investigators unable to tolerate ambiguity. Both would be sure to fail. Schon traces the foundations of policy in the study of the changing disciplines, the emergence of new scientific paradigms, and a willingness to undergo doubt and uncertainty in the search for institutional identity. Institutions need to tolerate conflict about their future and to endure the anguish of reexamination, and so, he argues, do social scientists whose efforts to study institutions cannot leave these processes out of account.

GENERAL FUNCTIONS OF SOCIETY

Responsiveness of Major Social Institutions to Cultural Expectations.
Ian H. Wilson, "Changing Values and Institutional Goals" (0001), 9 pp. Paper for the General Assembly of the World Future Society, Washington, D.C., 13 May 71. As social advance permits the most insistent needs to be met, those for biological and economic subsistence, their place will be taken by qualitative expectations. Only if they are substantially changed will institutions be able to serve these hitherto displaced goals, most notably the quality of life. "The current trouble—the trouble that puts so many of our institutions on a collision course with the future—is that they reflect almost exclusively organizational values such as order, routine, output, authority, efficiency. They reflect inadequately such other values as individualism, self-development, personal relationships, due process, equality." Mr. Wilson is Consultant on Business Environment to the General Electric Company.

Human Intelligence, Interdisciplinary Inquiry.

SYSTEMATICS, Journal of the Institute for the Comparative Study of History, Philosophy, and the Sciences (0002) . A quarterly journal of philosophy devoted to "the factors which influence development and retrogression in man and their operation in individuals and communities . . . general theories of man and his place in the universe . . . and comparative methodology in history, philosophy, and natural science." Annual rate $10.00 payable by dollar check, 5-7 Kingston Hill, Kingston-upon-Thames, Surrey, England.

Analysis of Policy Research Capability.

Richard H. Brown, Department of Sociology, University of California at San Diego, "Rationale for Creating a Capacity for Policy R&D on Broad Societal Issues" (0003) , unpublished paper. 13 pp., 1970. Recommends the establishment of multidisciplinary policy-oriented research centers to combine organizational expertise with knowledge in depth on substantive social problems. Describes the transformation of management consulting organizations resulting from the growth of knowledge.

Federal Government's Commitment to Academic Science.
President's Science Advisory Committee, *Scientific Progress, the Universities, and the Federal Government* (0004) (Washington, D.C.: The White House, 1960), v + 33 pp. Report of a Panel on Basic Research and Graduate Education, "The Seaborg Report."

Museum News.
(0005) Roberta Faul, Editor. Ten times yearly to members of the American Association of Museums, 2233 Wisconsin Avenue, N.W., Washington, D.C. 20007. $15.00 to non-members.

The Journal of Interdisciplinary History.
(0006) Editors, Robert I. Rotberg and Theodore K. Rabb, E53-490, Massachusetts

Institute of Technology, Cambridge, Mass. 02139. Quarterly, subscriptions $12.50 per year.

The Remote Prospect of a Humane Society.
Noam Chomsky, *Problems of Knowledge and Freedom; The Russell Lectures* (0007) (N.Y.: Pantheon Books, 1971), xi + 111 pp., $4.95. "In the modern world, the principle of growth in most men and women is hampered by institutions inherited from a simpler age," wrote Bertrand Russell, and in the first of the commemorative lectures at Trinity College, Cambridge, Chomsky progresses from an appreciation of his philosophy of knowledge to a sombre appraisal of the prospects for social change.

A Reinterpretation of the Youth Revolt as the Displacement of a Tired Elite.
Peter L. Berger and Brigitte Berger, "Room at the Top? The Blueing of America" (0008) , *The New Republic* (3 April 71), pp. 20-23. Interprets the oppositional culture of youth as a consequence of institutionalized childhood, "probably happier than any previous one in human society," that, not surprisingly, has developed a profound antagonism to the increasing bureaucratization of society. The Bergers contend that society will need increasing numbers of scientific, technical, and management personnel, and that those who spurn these opportunities will experience downward social mobility. "There is no reason to think that 'the system' will be unable to make the necessary accommodations. If Yale should become hopelessly greened, Wall Street will get used to recruits from Fordham and Wichita State. Italians will have no trouble running the RAND Corporation." Only if children of the lower-middle and working classes drop out would there be "literally no one left to mind the technological store." (p. 23)

Counseling: An Institutional Analysis.
Eli Ginzberg, *Career Guidance: Who Needs It, Who Provides It, Who Can Improve It* (0009) (N. Y.: McGraw-Hill, 1971) xv + 356 pp., bibliog., $7.95. The counseling establishment centered in high schools, oriented toward the field of psychology, devoted to keeping people in the stream of formal education, is here subjected to a broadly conceived historical and sociological analysis that finds its social responses sorely inadequate to the changing values of jobseekers and the changing characteristics of the job market. "Guidance can no longer continue to rely on dynamic psychology, not even on psychology itself. It must develop more sophisticated understanding of the sociology of institutions and the economics of the labor market. Manpower is a new discipline and, if the advances of the 1960's are projected, other advances will take place in the seventies which will underpin and give new direction to the work of guidance counselors. The sociology of institutions is both a matter of research and a matter of orientation. Systematic new knowledge will accumulate slowly,

but a more active orientation will enable guidance to use what it learns from its clients in a constructive fashion in feedback aimed at institutional reform." (pp. 327-38). Dr. Ginzberg is Director of the Conservation of Human Resources Project at Columbia University.

Structuring Interaction between Employers and Educators.
American Chemical Society and Manufacturing Chemists Association, "Towards Increased Understanding; A Report of a Conference on Academic-Industrial Relations Prepared as a Guide for Planning and Conducting Similar Conferences. 33 pp. Describes one means for bringing faculty and employers together. Without such mechanisms colleges will experience great difficulty in preparing students for a wider variety of careers. (0010)

General Systems.
(0011) Yearbook of the Society for General Systems Research. For information concerning membership in the society, subscriptions and back numbers of the Yearbook, write to the Business Office, Society for General Systems Research, Joseph Henry Building, Room 818, 2100 Pennsylvania Avenue, N.W., Washington, D.C. 20006.

GENERAL PURPOSE INSTITUTIONS

Institutional Change in U.S. Navy.
Henry Owen, "Institutional Reform: A Long, Hard Fight," (00001) *Washington Post*, 2 Mar 71, p. A16. Comments on institutional reform in the U.S. Navy between the World Wars and the role of Austin K. Doyle.

Existing Institutions—A Plea for Survival.
Alan Pifer, "The Jeopardy of Private Institutions" (00002), from *The Annual Report of the Carnegie Corporation of New York, for 1970*, pp. 3-15. Offers the following as arguments for continued financial support of private service institutions such as voluntary hospitals, colleges, and private secondary schools: they afford laymen avenues for civic involvement, they safeguard academic and professional freedom, they would be difficult to replace, and they diversity the national life. He recognizes that to millions of Americans "private institutions, like government itself, are simply part of what they consider a rotten system and of a status quo which they are convinced is entrenched against the kinds of social change they advocate. We cannot expect these Americans to be the defenders of the private commonweal enterprise unless ways are found to relate it far more effectively to their needs and aspirations; but how far it can go in this direction without at the same time alienating other constituencies and jeopardizing its financial support is an even more difficult question."

Quest for New Institutional Departures in the World of Learning.
Commission on the Year 2000, *The Future of Intellectual Institutions* (00003), record of plenary sessions, 1 and 2 Nov 68, 104 pp., American Academy of Arts and Sciences.

Organization for Social and Technical Innovations.
Documents describing work of the organization are available from 83 Rogers St.,
Cambridge, Mass. 02142. Donald A. Schon is Director. Program areas include
health, housing, education and training, crime control, transportation, and environmental planning. (0.02142)

Institute of Current World Affairs.
535 Fifth Ave., New York, New York 10017, established in 1926 to provide opportunity and financial assistance to a few persons of high character and unusual
promise to enable them to observe and study at first hand particular foreign areas,
their peoples, problems, and institutions. Newsletters written by the recipients of
fellowships are circulated privately to persons in government, education, business,
and the professions. (0.10017)

International Collaborative for Research and Education.
The World Institute, *Fields Within Fields. . .Within Fields: The Methodology of
the Creative Process* Published at intervals. Single issue price, $1.00 from the
Institute, 777 United Nations Plaza, New York, New York 10017. The World Institute is a nonprofit research and educational institution, serving the public,
counseling governments and educational institutions, and assisting research in
human ecology by grants and the exchange of ideas. It aspires to draw together
changing constellations of experts to integrate knowledge and techniques for the
advancement of third world peoples. Julius Stulman is President of the Institute's
Council. (0.10017)

The Manpower Institute. (0.20036)
1211 Connecticut Avenue, N.W., Washington, D.C. 20036. The Institute
has described its functions as follows: 1. To help assure appropriate action by education, industry, and government to achieve a better balance
between manpower supply and demand, particularly in professional and
technical areas which require long educational preparation; 2. To disseminate widely information on career opportunities, concentrating on
critical manpower areas; 3. To support research on key manpower issues not covered by the Bureau of Labor Statistics, the Engineers Joint
Council, the National Research Council's Board on Human Resources,
or other agencies.

The primary goal of The Institute is to develop programs of correc-
tive action rather than research. Its basic mission, within the context of
a free society, is to increase the probability of having the right number
of people, with the right skills, at the right place and at the right time to do
the nation's work. Many public manpower programs today focus under-
standably on urgently needed remedial programs for the disadvantaged.
However, very few aim at the solution of higher-level technical, professional, and skilled labor imbalances.

The Institutional Defense.
Subcommittee on Library and Memorials, Committee on House Administration, U.S. House of Representatives, *General Hearings on the Smithsonian Institution* (0.20560), July, 1970, 91st Congress, 2nd Session, 1032 pp. Critical sniping at the Smithsonian in the late 1960's prompted a Congressional review, to which the Institution responded with an extensive self-justification.

The Academy for Contemporary Problems.
505 King Avenue, Columbus, Ohio 43201. Brochure. (0.43201) "It is intended that the Academy will provide a new kind of focus for talents from all walks of national and international life to develop solutions to contemporary problems. While there are existing centers where technical specialists come together to address themselves to pressing public questions, the Academy will be a new kind of problem-solving institution—one in which the community-at-large will participate with experts in searching for solutions to the urgent challenges of contemporary society." Ralph R. Widner, Director.

Collaborative for Institutional Innovation

BLUEPRINT (Blueprint for Life and Understanding the Environment, Program of Research and Information for the New Times). (0.91105) A future-oriented collaborative devoted to institutional innovation. Nine active members, mostly in California at present, with the aid of a distinguished national advisory council, are developing plans for new organizations to respond to social problems. Robert V. Bartz, 231 Columbia Street, Pasadena, California 91105, serves as director. The present thrust is toward the development of a new action and planning framework at the community level.

Forum for Contemporary History.
(0.93102) P.O. Box 127, Stearns Wharf, Santa Barbara, California 93102. Bimonthly journal and biweekly letters from leaders of opinion seeking to take advantage of correspondence, a strongly protected area of freedom of expression under the First Amendment, to communicate views that the editors believe warrant extra protection as they tend to challenge established institutions. Founding membership, $18.00. James L. Bartlett, III, President-Publisher.

Center for the Study of Social Policy.
Stanford Research Institute, Menlo Park, California 94025. Dr. Willis W. Harman, Director, Charles W. Williams, Deputy Director. Outgrowth of the earlier Educational Policy Research Center, now oriented toward social policy generally. "Working Description," 5 pp. (0.94025).

CIDOC.
Centro Intercultural de Documentacion, Apartado 479, Cuernavaca, Mexico. Directed by Ivan Illich, this center conducts a far-reaching and wide-ranging program of explorations of cultural and social change in the Americas, well summarized in its publications and catalogues. (0. Mex..)

1. Universalization of Knowledge

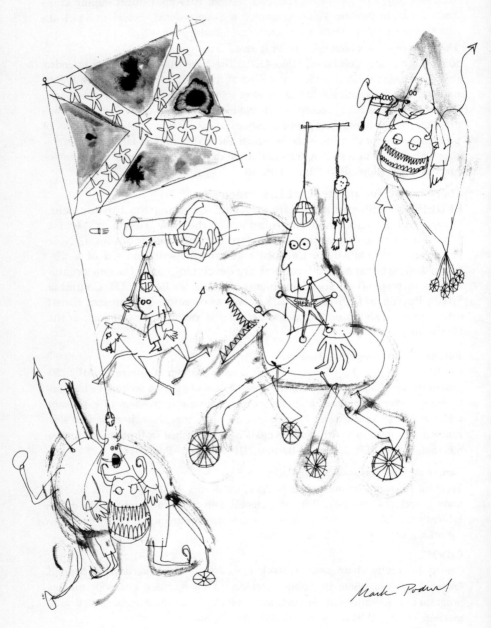

THE SILENT MAJORITY

Toward a Philosophy of Lifelong Learning.
CONVERGENCE: An International Journal of Adult Education (1000) Published quarterly. Subscriptions, $4.00 per year; P.O. Box 250, Station F, Toronto 5, Ontario, Canada. A journal of ideas with an international editorial committee, edited by J. Roby Kidd.

Learning in Contemporary Cultural Perspective.
Jerome S. Bruner, edited by Anita Gil, *The Relevance of Education* (1001) (N.Y.: W. W. Norton, 1971) xvi + 175 pp. "Mobilizing of knowledge in the interest of conviction that change is imperative. . ." can lead to "a vast change in our thinking about schools, about growth, about the assumption of responsibility in the technological world as we know it. I have wanted to highlight the role of intention and goal directedness in learning and the acquisition of knowledge, and the conversion of skill into the management of one's own enterprises. The objective is to produce skill in our citizens, skill in the achieving of goals of personal significance, and of assuring a society in which personal significance can still be possible." (p. 117)

INSTITUTIONS OF ELEMENTARY, SECONDARY, AND POPULAR EDUCATION

Changing the Public Resource Base of the Schools.
House Republican Task Force on Education and Training, "Property Tax: A Strained Base of Support" (10000), *Congressional Record,* 18 Jan 72, E1-28.

Effecting Change in Museum Practices.
F. Joseph Stokes, Jr., "Updating a Natural Science Museum; a Non-Professional Enthusiast Looks at Natural History Museums; Questions and Opinions" (10001), Dec 70, 34 pp. Not available for general circulation, but may be requested from the Academy of Natural Sciences, 19th & The Parkway, Philadelphia, Pa. 19103. A critical review of exhibition practice in 12 leading natural history museums by a trustee of the Academy of Natural Sciences of Philadelphia. Includes a checklist for exhibit planning.

Expanding Role of Museums in Science Education.
Smithsonian Institution, *Opportunities for Extending Museum Contributions to Pre-College Science Education; Summary Report of a Conference Supported by the National Science Foundation, January 26-27, 1970* (10002), 223 pp. incl. bibliography.

New Schools Exchange Newsletter.
Issued monthly. Five issues, $5.00, one-year subscription, including Directory of Schools, $10.00 in U.S. and $12.50 in Canada; 301 E. Canon Perdido, Santa Barbara, Calif. 93103. Over fifty numbers have been issued; includes job exchange (10003).

The Total Learning Population and Education Policy.
Stanley Moses, *The Learning Force: A More Comprehensive Framework for Educational Policy* (10004) Occasional Paper 25, Syracuse University Publications in Continuing Education. 37 pp. $1.25 from the Library of Continuing Education, 107 Roney Lane, Syracuse, N.Y. 13210. National education policy might extend beyond the traditional institutional "core" of schools and post-secondary institutions to include a vast "learning force" of individuals seeking educational experiences through extension, educational media, correspondence schools, churches, welfare agencies, and business, which Moses estimates to involve over 80 million participants.

Museum of the Media.
One Union Square West, New York, New York 10003. Stephen Globus is Director of Operations at this production center for mixed-media learning situations, which intends to distribute sets of slides and instructions for staging exhibits to schools, community organizations, and neighborhood centers. (1.10003)

Corporation for Public Broadcasting.
888 16th Street, N.W., Washington, D.C. 20006. *Newsletter.* (1.20006) Editor, Michael Ballard. Monthly.

Center for Research and Education.
P.O. Box 1768, Estes Park, Colorado 80517. Center (since relocated) devoted to language, cross-cultural communication, leadership, and ecology. Documents include fact sheets, program statements, and paper by Albert R. Wight, "Participative Education and the Inevitable Revolution" (1970). (1.80517)

2. Higher Education and Research

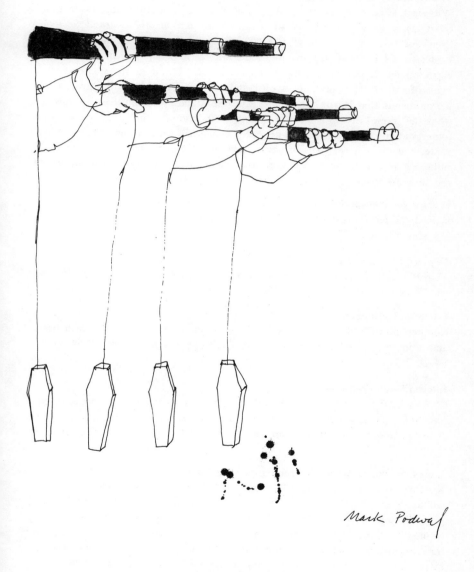

KENT STATE

Off-Campus Learning.
Donald J. Eberly, "An Agenda for Off-Campus Learning Experiences" (2000), Report of the Interlude Research Program, Menlo Park, California, Dec 69, 55 pp.

The Academy and Contemporary Problems.
William J. Bouwsma "Learning and the Problem of Undergraduate Education" (2001) in J. Voss and P.L. Ward, Eds., *Confrontation and Learned Societies* (New York University Press, 1970) $5.00. An article by a Renaissance historian, Professor of History at Harvard, about the implications for the academy of social expectations that undergraduate education will illuminate the contemporary crisis of values. "The problem is ultimately cultural, rather than educational." Recommends that learned societies "establish standing committees to consider what the several disciplines could contribute individually and collectively, to an undergraduate education that is primarily concerned with problems of meaning, value, and the general goals of our society, and then employ their considerable influence among scholars to convert the intellectual resources now confined to the separate disciplines to genuinely educational ends."

Science for Nonspecialists.
F. Reif, "Science Education for Nonscience Students" (2002), *Science,* Vol. 164 (30 May 69), pp. 1032-37.

Degrees by Examination.
Alan Pifer, "Is It Time for an External Degree?" (2003), *College Board Review,* no. 78 (Winter, 1970-71), pp. 5-10.

Peace and Education.
Congressman Charles Bennett, Remarks on need for an agency for world peace and undergraduate peace studies (2004), *Congressional Record,* 11 May 71, E4200-2.

International Education.
Charles E. Perry, President of Florida International University, address recommending world clearinghouse for the exchange of teachers, entered into the *Congressional Record* by Congressman Fascell of Florida, 11 Nov. 71, pp. E12090-92 (2005).

Limits on the University's Problem-Solving Role.
Kingman Brewster, Jr., "Yale University: 1969-70 The Report of the President" (2006) 15 Sep 70, 17 pp. Draws limits on the university's involvement in social problem solving, to preclude "the application of the known by the already trained." "If society tries to make the university become the vehicle for the current, operational solution of community problems, it may well sacrifice the one institution whose research and teaching is essential to the long-range fundamental solution of these same problems."

Undergraduate Education in Environmental Studies.
(2007) A conference report. The Public Affairs Center, Dartmouth College, Hanover, N.H. 03755 (Apr 70), 100 pp.

Reappraising the Social Role of Higher Education.
David C. Nichols, ed., "Papers Prepared for the Special Committee on Campus Tensions," *Perspectives on Campus Tensions* (2008) (Washington, D.C.: American Council on Education, 1970), ix + 219 pp., $3.50. The eruptions of campus violence are here bravely reinterpreted as reflecting a tension between the mindless allegiances of the contemporary university and the moral passions of its students.

Community-Based Off-Campus Learning.
Karen Duncan, "Community Action Curriculum Compendium" (2009), Report of the Community Action Curriculum Project, U.S. National Student Association, 16 Nov 68, 54 pp.

AAUP Bulletin.
(2010) Editor, Lawrence S. Poston, III, Department of English, University of Nebraska, Lincoln, Nebraska 68508. Subscriptions, $4.50, foreign $0.50 additional, from Suite 500, One Dupont Circle, N.W., Washington, D.C. 20036.

A Revolution on Behalf of Human Possibility.
John Hersey, *Letter to the Alumni* (2011) (N.Y.: Alfred A. Knopf and Bantam Books, 1970), 179 pp., paper, $1.25. Wise counsel from the novelist who served as Master of Pierson College at Yale for five years, asking for faith in higher education, and specifying some of the changes that institutions must make if they are to earn the faith of their students and the public at large.

Conference on Service-Learning.
Southern Regional Education Board, "Atlanta Service-Learning Conference Report" (2012), 130 6th St., N.W., Atlanta, Georgia 30313, 36 pp. Report of a 1970 conference; may be requested directly from the Board at the above address.

Proposal for a National Service System.
Congressman Jonathan B. Bingham, "A Limited National Service System: Replacing the Draft" (2013), *New Republic*, 16 Jan 71; reprinted in the *Congressional Record*, 4 Feb 71.

U.S. College Work-Study Program.
Congressman Michael Harrington, Remarks on College Work-Study Program (2014), *Congressional Record*, 14 June 71, pp. E5834-35. Call for an increase of $75.4 million for the program above the $442 million originally appropriated by the U.S. House of Representatives.

Changes in Cooperative Education.
J. Dudley Dawson, "New Directions for Cooperative Education" (2015), 15 Apr 71, 15 pp. Available from the National Commission for Cooperative Education, 52 Vanderbilt Ave., New York, New York 10017. Recent growth and future development of cooperative education programs seem limited by failures to involve faculty and inadequacies of employers' commitments to students. Also available, a list of 201 colleges and universities offering cooperative education programs.

Pathways toward Student Social Involvement.
National Service Secretariat, 5140 Sherrier Place, N.W., Washington, D.C. 20016. Donald Eberly, Director. *Newsletter,* quarterly (2016), $5.00.

The Accidental Structure of Academic Programs.
Leroy P. Richardson, National Laboratory for Higher Education Research Monograph no. 1, Mutual Plaza, Durham, North Carolina 27701, *Undergraduate Curriculum Improvement: A Conceptual and Bibliographic Study* (2017) 49 pp.

Institutional Alternatives in Education.
Michael Marien, *Alternative Futures for Learning; An Annotated Bibliography of Trends, Forecasts, and Proposals.* (2018) . Available from the Educational Policy Research Center, 1206 Harrison Street, Syracuse, New York 13210. 247 pp. 1971. $5.00. An extensive listing of books, bibliographies, and journal articles dealing with alternative visions of the future of education. Indexed by major author, organization, and selected subjects, with a separate index of bibliographies.

Instilling Social Allegiance Seen as College Goal.
John A. Howard, President, Rockford College; David Andrews, President, Principia College; Alexander Jones, President, Butler University; and Roy F. Ray, President, Friends University, "Report on the Present Circumstances of Higher Education" (2019), submitted to Robert H. Finch, Counselor to the President, Oct 70. Entered in the *Congressional Record,* 4 Nov 71, E11858-861 by Congressman Marvin Esch (R., Mich.). "The promotion of attitudes of affirmation, appreciation, and commitment, to counteract a prevailing enthusiasm for criticism and dissent" is recommended as "essential to the proper functioning of all higher education in this country."

Academic Institutions Part of Power System.
Alan Wolfe, "The Myth of the Free Scholar" (2020), *The Center Magazine,* Vol. 11, No. 4 (Jul 69) pp. 72-77. Charges that "unfreedom" arises in the university from its quest for social power, its dependence on external support, and "limitations of an institutional kind." Acceptance of conditions of scholarly work leads young academics to conform to institutional expectations.

Increasing the Emphasis on Teaching in Higher Education.
Committee on Undergraduate Teaching, The Hazen Foundation, 400 Prospect
Street, New Haven, Connecticut 06511. *The Importance of Teaching; A Memorandum to the New College Teacher* (2021) (1968), 86 pp.

Toward Change in the Education Function.
Ohmer Milton and Edward Joseph Shoben, Jr., *Learning and the Professors*
(2022) (Ohio University Press, 1968) xvii + 216 pp., $2.95.

Objectives and Character of the Private University.
Douglas Brown, *The Liberal University: An Institutional Analysis* (2023) N.Y.:
McGraw-Hill, 1969).

University Goals—A Commentary.
C.G. Dobbins and C.B.T. Lee, eds. *Whose Goals for American Higher Education?*
(2024) (Washington, D.C.: American Council on Education, 1968), $6.00. 241 pp.

Differing Goal Emphasis of Institutions.
S. D. Sieber et al., *A Taxonomy of Higher Education* (2025) (N.Y.: Bureau of
Applied Social Research, Columbia University, March, 1968).

Our Institutions Reshape Us and We Then Reshape Them.
A. H. Halsey and M. A. Trow, *The British Academics* (2026) (Harvard University
Press, 1971) 560 pp. Describes four differing professional orientations on the part
of British faculty members (elitist researchers, elitist teachers, expansionist researchers, and expansionist teachers), each yielding different institutional prescriptions. Includes thoughtful analysis of the sources of change and of resistance
to change among them.

A Growing Awareness of Institutional Consequences of Federal Research Support.
U.S. House of Representatives, Committee on Government Operations, *Conflicts
between the Federal Research Programs and the Nation's Goals for Higher Education* (2027) (89th Congress, 1st Session, 1965), House Report No. 1158, Hearings, and "Responses from the Academic and Other Interested Communities...,"
2 vols.

Black Aspirations and Higher Education.
W. Todd Furniss *et al.*, "Background Papers for Participants at the 52nd Annual
Meeting of the American Council on Education," *The Campus and the Racial
Crisis* (2028) (Washington, D.C.: American Council on Education, 1969), 139 pp.

Study Commissions on Higher Education.
Morris Norfleet and Dan Coleman, "Higher Education under the

Microscope" (2029). Paper for the American Association of State Colleges and Universities. July, 1971, 11 pp. Lists directors, purpose, program, source of support, and members of eight major study groups: the Commission on Non-traditional Study, the Commission on Academic Affairs, the National Commission on the Future of State Colleges and Universities, the Carnegie Commission on Higher Education, the Newman Task Force, the Committee to Explore Exemplary Innovations in Post-Secondary Education, a Study on Restructuring Higher Education, and the Assembly on University Goals and Governance.

Loss of Institutional Autonomy.
John Walsh, "California Higher Education: The Master Plan Faulted" (2030), *Science,* Vol.164 (16 May 69), pp.811-13. The advent of centralized state planning for higher education is traced to "the pathology of the present situation" in California, in which political factors are seen to loom large.

New Lives Cannot Follow Old Lines.
Judson Jerome, *Culture Out of Anarchy; The Reconstruction of American Higher Learning* (2031) (N.Y.: Herder and Herder, 1970), xxii + 330 pp., $9.50. Jerome's interpretation of contemporary change in experimental colleges is based upon seventeen years' teaching experience in them. Educational reform has made very little progress toward defining or achieving its goals and that has been very painful for students and faculty alike, judging from his descriptions of six pioneering institutions. He charges that the established system of higher education seems to be designed to select students out, like a thruway from which most cars must exit, leaving only a few to continue on to the graduate schools, as though their entry were the goal for which the system was engineered. "The most common charge against the educational establishment is that we are trying to prepare young people to fit into slots." (p. 85) Each student's search for meaning and value should be the primary determinant of the system, even if this means that some of its proudest institutions should dissolve. "The principle underlying educational reform is that institutions should exist to serve people, not to shape them." (p. 330)

Seeking Out the Gifted.
Dael Wolfle, ed., The Walter Van Dyke Bingham Lectures on the Development of Exceptional Abilities and Capacities, *The Discovery of Talent* (2032) (Harvard University Press, 1969), xxii + 316 pp., $9.50. Concentrating with a few exceptions on persons manifesting high intelligence, the authors in this series discuss means of recognizing such talent and preventing its loss. In less academic fields, such as architecture, the subject of a 1962 lecture by Donald W. Mackinnon, creativity does not bear so close a relationship to formally manifested intelligence.

Those who were later most creative were profoundly skeptical as students and often rebellious. "We would do well then to pay more attention in the future than we have in the past to the nurturing of those nonintellective traits which in our studies have been shown to be intimately associated with creative talent." (pp. 206-7)

Institutional Appraisal of a Field of Study.
Claude Welch, *Graduate Education in Religion; A Critical Appraisal* (2033) (University of Montana Press, 1971), xx + 279 pp. An unusually thoughtful survey of higher education in religion, its relationship to the professions it serves, and the improvements required. It recommends that the number of graduate departments be reduced and that enrollments be cut back by one third, while at the same time strengthening the interrelationships between religious studies and other university programs. "Devices are badly needed for overall planning in the use of resources and for the allocation of responsibility for the development of particular fields of specialization. It is not enough to say there is a need for more rational planning among institutions. For there has been simply none at all. Each institution has proceeded in its own way, usually without consultation and always without review by others, and with insufficient attention to the question of what an institution is able to do distinctively." (p. 6)

Social Character of the Research Endeavor.

John Ziman, *Public Knowledge: The Social Dimension of Science* (2034) (Cambridge University Press, 1968) 147 pp., paper, $1.95. Science is essentially a form of "public knowledge." For the scientist, "the absolute need to communicate one's findings, to make them acceptable to other people, determines their intellectual form." Most scientists give their allegiance not to formal scientific associations but rather to an informal institution which is comprised of scientists in the same field studying the same problems—an informal association of which one becomes a member through patronage, through being connected with the "big names" in the field. It is of maximum importance for a scientist to gain acceptance of his ideas by his peers. He is therefore committed to the consensus principle, in favor of which controversy is muted and there are no strong challenges to another's ideas. This search for peer group approval, this striving for a public consensus, takes precedence over the strict application of the scientific method. Professor Ziman maintains that most pure scientists have little concern for the major purposes of the corporation or institution which employs them, and they seek to avoid any administrative involvement in institutions in order to devote all of their time to the research function, through which they maintain their standing in the scientific community. The author is professor of theoretical physics at the University of Bristol.

International Study of Education Policy.
Irving J. Spitzberg, Newsletters for the Institute of Current World Affairs, (2035), 535 Fifth Avenue, New York, N.Y. 10017, to which requests for copies may be addressed.

The Search for Vocation.
Robert J. Ginn, Jr., "NEW DIRECTIONS, A Guide to Opportunities in the Area of Social Change and Other Vocational Alternatives" (2036) (Harvard University: Office for Graduate and Career Plans, 1970) 36 pp., mimeo., distribution limited. Searching guide for graduates seeking employment in social action, social welfare, education, and alternative institutions.

Graduate Education in Science.
National Science Foundation, *Toward a Public Policy for Graduate Education in the Sciences* (2037) (Washington: U.S. Government Printing Office, 1969) 0-328-298, 79 pp. $.40. Statistics and analyses published separately as *Graduate Education: Parameters for Public Policy* (2038) (Washington: U.S. Government Printing Office) 0-331-173, 180 pp., $1.25.

Established Institutions and Equal Opportunity.
Bernard C. Watson, "Survival Phase II: Unity without Uniformity" (2039), *Congressional Record,* 18 Aug 72, H8016-22. Alternative institutions are untried instruments for the advancement of minorities, whose best hope may be to increase the effectiveness of mainstream institutions. An excellent summary of education and the black community presented to the National Urban League convention in July of 1972.

Equity and Racism as Poles of Institutional Performance.
Elias Blake, Jr., "Higher Education for Black Americans: Issues in Achieving More than Just Equal Opportunity" (2040), *Congressional Record,* 3 May 72, E4615-19.

Higher Education in the Social Setting.
Alan Pifer, "The Responsibility for Reform in Higher Education" (2041), *Congressional Record,* 29 Mar 72, S5119-122. Reprinted from the *Annual Report of the Carnegie Corporation for 1971.* Advocates ameliorative measures that would reduce the burdens on higher education, and argues that these should be undertaken on a system-wide basis. Doubts that "unilateral action by higher education to reduce its range of functions and activities sharply, thereby 'purging' itself and reverting to the only 'proper' pursuits—teaching and scholarly research" would be a feasible approach to reform. "It runs so contrary to the American concept of higher education in society, especially public higher education, as to be quite unrealistic and impractical as a way of reforming the *system,* however attractive it may be to an occasional individual institution."

Postdoctoral Investigators.
National Academy of Science, *The Invisible University: Postdoctoral Education in the United States* (2042)(1969), xxii + 310 pp. Although not undertaken as an inquiry into changing institutional patterns of higher education, this study of postdoctoral training on and off campus describes student interchange at the advanced level and offers a sketch of an emerging institutional system.

Institutionalizing Waste in Research.
Paul Dickson, "The Empire of Think Tanks" and "Making the Intolerable Tolerable", the first reprinted from *The Progressive* (Nov 71) and the second from *Book World* (31 Oct 71) in the *Congressional Record* for 3 Nov 71 (2043) , entered with remarks by Senator Mansfield, S17522-25. Senator Mansfield and Paul Dickson, both critics of military research, have now turned their fire on "think tanks," by which they mean contract research centers supported by government agencies, but the term is vague and might lead to damaging losses of confidence in other independent and governmental establishments. Dickson's charges that such centers lower the quality of research are imprecise.

Federal Higher Education Programs of the Sixties.
"Major Johnson Higher Education Papers" (2044), *The Chronicle of Higher Education*, 7 Feb 72, pp. 3-7. Includes education sections from the 1964 report of a task force chaired by John Gardner which laid the basis for the Higher Education Act of 1965, a 1966 interagency task force, and 1967 proposals of a task force headed by William C. Friday, President of the University of North Carolina.

Military Ties Jeopardize Future of American Higher Education.
Lord Bowden, "Universities and Society" (2045), *New Scientist*, 26 Mar 70, pp. 601-3. The author, Principal of the Institute of Science and Technology of the University of Manchester, contends that "American universities have come to rely more and more heavily and to a dangerous degree on funds from the Pentagon.... The Americans must find another way of financing their universities, or they may be destroyed by the horror of Vietnam." (p. 602)

Doctor of Arts Degree.
Arthur M. Eastman, "One New Trend in Graduate Education" (2046), draft introduction to a report on the Doctor of Arts degree, forthcoming from the Council of Graduate Schools in the United States, One Dupont Circle, N.W., Washington, D.C. 20036. 17 pp.

A Prescient Call for Sociocultural Analysis of Institutions.
Robert S. Lynch, *Knowledge for What? The Place of Social Science in American Culture* (2047) (Princeton University Press, 1939), reprinted, paper, 1967, ix + 268 pp., $2.45. A re-issue of this much-admired book serves as a reminder that over thirty years ago Professor Lynch called for

greater receptivity to institutional change; interdisciplinary research, especially on urban problems; and "a culture that in all its institutions will play down the need for and the possibility of war." "Our task here as social scientists is to try to discover what sort of culture that culture would be which utilized its best intelligence systematically at point after point to plan to coordinate the institutionalized ways of doing things which are important to us as persons. (p. 209) Urged that institutions be studied as instruments of the total culture.

The Shrinking Academic Job Market.
Allan M. Cartter, "Scientific Manpower for 1970-1985" (2048), *Science,* Vol. 172 (9 April 71), pp. 132-140. Unless positive steps are taken to encourage early retirement and postpone the award of tenure, Cartter believes that the award of Ph.D.'s to those already seeking the degree will satisfy all or virtually all academic employment needs by 1985. He recommends coordination of professional society manpower planning by an appropriate private organization such as the American Association for the Advancement of Science. He cautions that federal support of graduate education has typically been predicted on forecasts of manpower shortages and argues that a new rationale for such support is urgently needed.

Institutional Strains from the Oversupply of Ph.D.'s.
Dael Wolfle and Charles V. Kidd, "The Future Market for Ph.D.'s" (2049), *Science,* Vol. 173 (27 Aug 71), pp. 784-793. The authors leave no room for hope that the present institutional structure can employ the graduates it produces. They also recognize that departments which should be pruned will resist cutbacks in graduate admissions. One remedy which the authors do not propose would be to consolidate applicants in pools by fields, admit to the pool the number assigned to that field by a review board on human resources, and then let the universities compete for them. The authors concede that "inter-institutional tensions" are inevitable. The question is whether constructive methods for the redeployment of talent can be devised and put into effect.

Creating Jobs for Ph.D.'s.
Frederick E. Terman, "Supply of Scientific and Engineering Manpower: Surplus or Shortage" (2050), *Science,* Vol. 173 (30 July 71), pp. 399-405.

Likelihood of Ph.D. Oversupply in 1980.
National Science Foundation, *1969 & 1980 Science & Engineering Doctorate Supply & Utilization* (2051) (U.S.G.P.O. 1971-0-425-954) 32 pp., $0.50.

Professional Interests and Learned Societies.
Deborah Shapley, "Professional Societies: Identity Crisis Threatens on Bread and Butter Issues" (2052), *Science*, Vol. 176 (19 May 72), pp. 777-79.

Proposal: Limit Graduate Admissions to Level of Jobs.
History of Science Society, minutes of business meeting, 29 Dec 71, defeating a resolution to urge graduate departments "to matriculate in any academic year no more than the average number of students they have successfully placed in positions commensurate with their training (teaching, research, curatorships, etc.) in the last three years." (2053)

Caution on the Employment Outlook.
American Philosophical Association, "Memorandum to Prospective Graduate Students in Philosophy from the Board of Officers, 30 Sept 71" (2054), cautions that the number of academic vacancies will be less than the number of Ph.D. recipients in future. "We are distributing this statement not in order to discourage really well-qualified students from going into philosophy, but simply in order to urge them to gather the fullest possible information and to make realistic plans."

Technical Unemployment.
National Science Foundation, Science Resources Studies Highlights, "Unemployment Rates for Scientists, Spring 1971," 4 pp., and "Unemployment Rate for Engineers, June-July 1971," 4 pp. (2055). Reports an unemployment rate of 2.6 percent for scientists (up from 1.5 percent the year before) and 3.0 percent for engineers (up from 1.6 percent the year before).

Proposal: Force Departments to Retain Surplus Ph.D.'s.
The Arden House Group, American Physical Society, "Proposal" (2056) that graduate student support funds be diverted to sustain unemployed Ph.D. recipients, thus cutting back departments' capacities to support additional candidates. Offered at the 1971 meeting of the American Physical Society.

Other Institutions, Other Careers.
Louis Kampf, "'It's Alright, Ma (I'm Only Bleeding)': Literature and Language in the Academy" (2057), *PMLA*, Vol. 87 (1972), pp. 377-383. Presidential Address to the Modern Language Association calling for a new professional orientation, away from institutions which "are part of a rationalized arrangement for the profitable use of knowledge."

The Academic Bubble.
Lewis B. Mayhew, "An Essay Written for the Carnegie Commission on Higher Education," *Graduate and Professional Education, 1980; A Sur-*

vey of Institutional Plans (2058) (N.Y.: McGraw-Hill, 1970) x + 38 pp., $3.95. Institutional momentum toward new graduate programs is increasing despite the forecasted downturn in future academic employment. "If such expectations are realized, the first and most obvious implication is the possibility of an oversupply of potential college teachers holding the doctorate." (p. 28)

The Science Doctorate Population.
Lindsay Harmon, "Career Patterns Report No. 1," *Profiles of Ph.D.'s in the Sciences; Summary Report on Follow-up of Doctorate Cohorts, 1935-1960* (2059) (Washington, D.C.; National Academy of Sciences, 1965) x + 123 pp., $2.50.

Nonacademic Employment; A Preliminary Appraisal.
Lindsay R. Harmon, "Career Patterns Report No. 1," *Profiles of Ph.D.'s Academic versus Nonacademic; A Second Report on Follow-up of Doctorate Cohorts 1935-1960* (22029) (Washington, D.C.: National Academy of Sciences, 1968) xi + 106 pp.

Research and Development: Funding and Employment.
National Science Foundation, *National Patterns of R&D Resources; Funds & Manpower in the United States 1953-1972* (2061) (NSF 72-300, U.S.G.P.O. 3800-0112) vi + 34 pp., $0.50. An easy-to-use summary of the deployment of technical manpower resources in research and development. 519,000 scientists and engineers were employed in research and development in 1971, down five percent from 1970. Since 1964 the percentage of scientists and engineers engaged in research and development has dropped from over 37 percent to about 35 percent.

Worsening Outlook for University Employment.
James Harvey, "Ph.D.'s and the Marketplace" (2062) ERIC Higher Education Research Currents, 1 Feb 72, 4 pp., $0.15. Concise review of recent forecasts of declining academic employment opportunities for Ph.D.'s.

Training Agents of Institutional Change.
"A Business School for Entrepreneurs of Change" (2063), *Business Week* (25 Apr 70). Describes program at Vanderbilt University Graduate School of Management. See PROMETHEUS, One/three, p. 69.

The Ecology of Academic Careerism.
Theodore Caplow and Reece J. McGee, *The Academic Marketplace* (2064) (N.Y.: Doubleday Anchor Books, 1965), x + 226 pp. The marketplace is the environment wherein academic careers are shaped. Although first published in 1958, this study has still not been properly appreciated

and may be read with profit by anyone seeking the ugly reality behind the facades of academic employment.

Proposal: An Academic Register.
David G. Brown *The Mobile Professors* (2065) (Washington, D.C.: American Council on Education, 1967), xi + 212 pp. Economic analysis of a survey of 13,000 newly hired faculty members, affords a rationale for establishing a bulletin of academic vacancies and a national register of individuals seeking academic positions.

Economic Incentives and Career Choice.
Richard B. Freeman *The Market for College-Trained Manpower; A Study in the Economics of Career Choice* (2066) (Harvard University Press, 1971), xxvi + 264 pp., $10.00. Economic incentives appear to be adequate means of reorienting the career plans of college students, although many improvements could be made in information available about opportunities. Freeman's formulation does not suppose that all or even most jobseekers are influenced by economic considerations, only that enough are, especially on the borderlines between careers, so that increasing salary levels and providing educational subsidies may reliably be expected to recruit additional jobseekers.

Colloquium on Prospects for Science Ph.D.'s.
Sanborn C. Brown and Brian B. Schwartz, eds., "M.I.T. Reports No. 22," *Scientific Manpower; A Dilemma for Graduate Education* (2067) (M.I.T. Press, 1971) x + 180 pp., $5.95. Composite estimate of the future of employment opportunity for Ph.D.'s in the sciences, with particular reference to difficulties created for educational institutions by fluctuations in governmental support for research.

Teaching Enhancement; Institutional Change is Needed.
Kenneth E. Eble, Director, Project to Improve College Teaching, 1259 East Temple, Salt Lake City, Utah 84102, *The Recognition and Evaluation of Teaching* (2068), 111 pp., $1.00. Also available from the AAUP, One Dupont Circle, N.W., Washington, D.C. 20036. Bibliography and appendices. While this is not an analysis in institutional terms it centers on the relationship between the professional values fostered by institutions and the performance of faculty members.

Social Service Motivation.
National Center for Information on Careers in Education, *Youth and Careers in Education* (2060) (N.Y.: Hill and Knowlton, 1971), 187 pp. Reports on a survey of nearly ten thousand high school and college students about career plans. The principal finding is that today's student expects to play a role in social change. The job value of greatest importance to all students surveyed was being helpful to others or useful to so-

ciety. Thirty per cent of college students and ten percent of high school students viewed the present role of education in society as being "to insure the maintenance of the ideas, beliefs, and values of the present society," while only four percent of the former and nine per cent of the latter considered education to be "a system to help young people to change society and build a new, improved world." (p. 26) Skepticism as to the social value of education makes some students reluctant to enter the field.

The Overeducated Society, a Diagnosis.

John K. Folger, Helen S. Astin, and Alan E. Bayer, "Staff Report of the Commission on Human Resources and Advanced Education," *Human Resources and Higher Education* (2070) (N.Y.: Russell Sage Foundation, 1970), xxxii + 475 pp., $17.50. This massive volume summarizes a large number of manpower studies in order to arrive at appraisals of the market for educated workers, not only in a series of fields ranging from welfare to the performing arts but also in terms of structural features such as mobility and professionalism. It may serve as an excellent introduction to the manpower situation as conceived by educational researchers and other academic observers in the late 60's. Especially it reveals the assumptions of manpower planning: confident where numbers of students and graduates show good correlations with specific occupational populations, much less confident where this is not so. Predicting that the number of college graduates will continue to outpace needs, the authors advocate absorbing them by raising the educational requirements of occupations whose entrants have not heretofore been expected to have a college degree. They observe at one point that "the problem of redirecting the voluntary choices of today's youth is formidable." (p. 13) Is the problem one of redirecting choice or undertaking the institutional changes required to accommodate aspirations? On the latter point this book is silent—damning testimony to the conventions that have for so long dominated thinking about human resources. The educational system appears as a fractional distillation process in which more or less volatile quantities are drawn in expectation of satisfying demand for occupational fuel. Occupational redefinition, job creation, and social change do not figure in plans for the system, which is tantamount to saying that they have been designed out.

Unemployment—A Preventive Remedy.

Herbert E. Striner, "Studies in Employment and Unemployment," *Continuing Education as a National Capital Investment* (2071) (Washington, D.C.: The W. E. Upjohn Institute for Employment and Research, 1972), x + 118 pp. $1.25 from publications office, Upjohn Institute, 300 South Westnedge Avenue, Kalamazoo, Mich. 49007. Prompted by the inadequacies of unemployment insurance in fostering job transition or remedying unemployment among youth, Striner studied the role of government in providing retraining in France, Germany, and Denmark. The German Employment Promotion Act of 1969 and Law No. 71-575 of France, "pertaining to the organizing of continuous professional training within the framework of continuing education" are printed in translation in appendices. Recommends the conversion of all state unemployment insurance funds as a "National Economic Security Fund," supporting a sophisticated array of retraining programs. The search for institutional innovations in Europe and their translation into recommendations tailored to the American setting is a commendable procedure.

The Journal of Human Resources.
Quarterly. (2072) Published under the auspices of the Industrial Relations Research Institute, the Center for Studies in Vocational and Technical Education, and the Institute for Research on Poverty of the University of Wisconsin. Editor: Robert J. Lampman. Annual rate $8.00 for individuals and $16.00 for institutions; foreign subscriptions add $0.50. Journals Department, University of Wisconsin Press, P.O. Box 1379, Madison, Wisconsin 53701.

Integration of Work and Education.
Sidney P. Marland, Jr., "Career Education—A New Frontier" (2073) , *Congressional Record* (14 Dec 71), E13401-4. Of 3.7 million young people leaving the formal educational system in 1970-71, 850,000 dropped out before finishing high school, 750,000 graduated from high school with little or nothing to offer prospective employers, and 850,000 dropped out of college before completing the program in which they had enrolled. Dr. Marland estimates that this group represents one-third of all educational expenditures: "We spend billions (nearly 28 yearly) to prepare 2.5 million young people for potential disenchantment, aimlessness, and failure, year after year after year." (E13402) Recommends reorientation of federal education programs to widen preparation for the job market in secondary and post-secondary education.

Structural Change for Upward Mobility.
S. M. Miller, "Strategies for Reducing Credentialism" (2074) , *Good Government* (Summer 70), pp. 10-13. Learning gained on the job should become a credential for advancement or at least access to opportunities for further study. One concept, offered by Sumner Rosen, would bridge the gulf that separates dead-end jobs from those that lead upward. Another, offered by the author and Frank Riessman, would connect work and education much more closely. "The idea is to construct a job structure which has stepping stones at all points in the life cycle rather than fixed and enduring places for individuals. . .Reducing credentialism implies continuous development and reshaping of the abilities of individuals, a move from emphasis on school certification to occupational de-

velopment, and, most importantly, investment in the worth and potential of all." Although the author does not so state, a corollary of his proposals might be to establish lines of vocational opportunity in which technological demands are muted and wider scope is afforded to manual and interpersonal skills.

Educated Workers, The Demand Will Be Saturated.
Eli Ginzberg, "The Outlook for Educated Manpower" (2075), *The Public Interest*, No. 26 (Winter 72), pp. 100-111. Colleges will absorb fewer and fewer Ph.D.'s in the 1970's and the economy seems unlikely to expand rapidly enough to create employment opportunities for this group in the private sector. "While the labor force as a whole will increase twenty percent between 1968 and 1980, the number with bachelor's degrees will increase just under 50 percent, those with master's degrees about 100 percent, and those with doctorates over 115 percent. Since seven out of 10 new degree recipients are expected to enter the civilian labor force during these 12 years. . .the proportion of educated persons seeking employment will be far higher than in any previous decade." (p. 107)

Social Program Evaluation Research.
Albert D. Biderman and Laure M. Sharp, *The Competitive Evaluation Research Industry* (2076) Bureau of Social Science Research, Inc., 1200 17th Street, N.W., Washington, D.C. 20036, 75 pp.

Reorienting the Teachers' Colleges.
American Association of State Colleges and Universities, "AASCU Studies 1971/5" *Today's Education for Tomorrow's Jobs* (2077) (Dec 71). iv + 92 pp., $3.00 from the association, One Dupont Circle, Washington, D.C. 20036.

Changing Employment Practices on Behalf of Women.
Commission on the Status of Women in the Profession, Modern Language Association, Report on Affirmative Action for Women in 1971 (2078), *PMLA*, Vol. 87 (1972), pp. 530-540. Unequal treatment of women has been a consequence of the customary cronyism of the academic job market. Where departments make an effort to find qualified women as candidates for appointment they seem readily able to do so, according to this survey of 247 departments.

Institutional Analysis of the American University.
Joseph Ben-David, Essays Sponsored by The Carnegie Commission on Higher Education, *American Higher Education; Directions Old and New* (2079) (N.Y.: McGraw-Hill, 1972), xv, 137 pp., $5.95. This masterful survey of the American institutional system of higher education deals with

education, training, and research—their dynamic interactions and the unstable equilibrium among them which has thrown the contemporary university off balance. The failure of so many commentators to deal with the university as a research institution—the major social role of many universities and the predominant cost in some— has greatly lessened the practical applicability of their ideas. Ben-David's interpretation of some graduate student populations as "a submerged proletarian class created inadvertently by the demand for research workers by the new research enterprises at the universities" (p. 109) is chilling. He condemns as utopian the notion that all university faculty members must be publishing research scholars or scientists. He advocates a shift toward vocational orientations in much undergraduate instruction and greater opportunity to interrupt the educational sequence in order to work, tending to reverse the usual progression from the abstract to the practical which probably frustrates the curiosity of many of today's students. He ably identifies the factors that have led to the politicization of the university and considers that the principal effect of such a transformation would not be a decline in teaching ("a university guided by political doctrine need not necessarily be an intellectually unexciting place" p. 124) but the loss of the university's role in scientific research, which would then be assumed by academies and various kinds of other establishments.

Counselor's Information Service.
Quarterly list of publications, issued by B'nai B'rith Vocational Service, 1640 Rhode Island Avenue, N.W., Washington, D.C. 20036. Editor: Dr. S. Norman Feingold. Annual rate $7.00. Categories include vocational information, guidance, student aids, aids for teachers, books, etc. (2080)

Higher Education: Systemic Failings.
Warren Bennis, "Education: Present and Future" (2081), *Congressional Record,* 27 Sept 71, S15104-8. Higher education, in Bennis's view, has become too large and lost its proper relationship to the world of work. Bennis is highly regarded as a student of contemporary management and assumed the presidency of the University of Cincinnati in September of 1971.

Institutions and Teaching Effectiveness.
Jerry G. Gaff and Robert C. Wilson, "The Teaching Environment; A Study of Optimum Working Conditions for Effective College Teaching" (2082), (1971), 67 pp. Available from the Center for Research and Development in Higher Education, University of California, Berkeley, California 94720. Effective teaching is found to depend upon environmental factors which individual institutions are urged to provide.

Ending Sex Discrimination in Academic Employment.
J. Stanley Pottinger, Director, Office for Civil Rights, U.S. Department of Health, Education, and Welfare, Remarks to the Panel on Affirmative Action and Faculty Policy, American Association of University Professors, 5 May 72 (23 pp.); Executive Order 11246 as amended; 41 *Code of Federal Regulations* 60.2 and 60.20, "Affirmative Action Programs" and "Sex Discrimination Guidelines." In Pottinger's words, "Neither do I understand academic freedom to be a justification for making faculties into men's clubs, entrenched in their 'old Boy' methods of recruitment. . . and irrationally resistant to the prospects of any change in the university's employment policies." (2083)

War Chest for Professional Enhancement.
American Chemical Society, "Professional Enhancement Program" (2084) , *Chemical & Engineering News* (14 Feb 72, 27 March 72). President-elect Alan Nixon was nominated by petition on a platform proposing vigorous action to improve employment opportunities. At his prompting, the Council of the ACS approved a $10 annual assessment of the membership to raise a fund for professional enhancement: direct support to unemployed members, increased employment aid activities, lobbying for more support for chemistry, and development of internship and job creation programs.

Talent Mobilization for Social Needs.
Ellis R. Mottur, "Monograph No. 8," *Conversion of Scientific and Technical Resources: Economic Challenge—Social Opportunity* (2085) . $3.00 from the Program of Policy Studies, The George Washington University, Washington, D.C. 20006. Proposes that the technical capabilities of the nation be mobilized for a massive effort at urban renovation and the creation of new cities, that incentives be offered to render the civilian sector more responsive to research and development and such research and development more responsive to social needs. Recommends a national policy favoring the goal of assured opportunities for socially useful employment for scientists and engineers, sustained by a major National Science Foundation program of continuing education in science and technology. Suggests that federal funds for research and development be set at a percentage of GNP by a national commission and that another commission be established to oversee the conversion of financial and manpower resources from military to civilian purposes.

Plea for an Institutional System Plan for Research.
Paul L. Dressel and Donald R. Come, *Impact of Federal Support of Science on the Publicly Supported Universities and Four-Year Colleges in Michigan* (2086) (Michigan State University, 1969) viii + 135 pp. Available in limited supply from the principal author. State support for public colleges and universities is normally predicated on a comprehensive plan assigning specific roles to individual insti-

tutions. This technique contrasts sharply with the project system used by the Federal Government for the support of sponsored research. The authors concluded from a two-year study of twelve public institutions in Michigan that the conflict between systems for research support has greatly impaired institutional autonomy.

Need for Stability and Continuity in Academic Research.
Carl M. York, "Steps toward a National Policy for Academic Science" (2087), *Science,* 14 May 71, pp. 643-48. Urges more continuity in research support and stabilizing level of support for graduate students.

Career Education—Ingredients of Governmental Commitment.
U.S. Senator Robert C. Byrd, "Career Education—An Idea Whose Time Has Come" (2088), *Congressional Record,* 25 May 72, S8455-57.

Supplanting Departments in the University.
Dael Wolfle, "The Supernatural Department" (2089), *Science,* Vol. 173 (9 July 71), editorial. Identifying the department with a reductionist approach in science (a suggestion that merits elaboration), Wolfle argues that science can best be advanced in coming years by a synthetic approach that will require new organizational forms. "Universities are under severe financial, political, and intellectual stress; disadvantageous as that stress is in other respects, it is in times of crisis that new procedures and organizational forms are likely to be accepted, for it is then that outworn habits are most easily broken."

Unionization of Faculty.
Myron Lieberman, "Professors Unite!" (2090), *Harpers,* Oct 71, pp. 61-70.

Six University Presidents' Paper on Issues.
Glenn S. Dumke et al., "Selected Problems Facing Higher Education in the 70's" (2091) *Congressional Record,* 21 April 72, E4135-140. In this report to Presidential Counselor Robert Finch the presidents of six public universities plead for stability and a recovery of public confidence in higher education. Implicitly they reject the thesis that fundamental change is required, so their statement is an interesting document of the point of view which proponents of change must usually challenge.

INSTITUTIONS OF HIGHER EDUCATION AND RESEARCH

Comparative Study of Research Establishments.
Joseph Ben-David, *Fundamental Research and the Universities: Some Comments on International Differences* (20000), (1968), 111 pp. Publication No. 23569 of the Organisation for Economic Cooperation and Development; OECD Publications, 2 rue Andre Pascal, Paris XVI, or OECD Publications Center, 1750 Pennsylvania Ave. N.W., Suite 1305, Washington, D.C. 20006.

The Russian Research Establishment—A Comparative View.

R.W. Davies and R. Amann, "Science Policy in the U.S.S.R." (20001), *Scientific American,* Vol. 220, No. 6 (June 69), pp. 19-29. A reappraisal indicating that the U.S.S.R. operates a research establishment comparable in size to that of the U.S. and that there are few substantial differences between these national systems.

Academic Institutions Losing Autonomy.

Walter P. Metzger, "Academic Freedom in Delocalized Academic Institutions" (20003) in Metzger et al., *Dimensions of Academic Freedom* (University of Illinois Press, 1969), pp. 1-33. An analysis of the influence of the institutional system of higher education on the *General Report on Academic Freedom and Academic Tenure* (1915), with particular emphasis on the "localness" of the college or university early in this century. The process of "delocalization" has been accompanied by a rise in coordination from without, a loss of internal authority, and widening influence for courts and other public bodies. Asserts that government sponsorship of academic research serves to "rob the university of autonomy". (p. 23) "Almost any agency out to promote an unpleasant mission can find a pretext for lodging it in the university, to acquire gilt by association." (p. 25).

"At the top of the list of credos ripe for change I would put the view that a crime against academic freedom is a crime against an academic person's rights. In relevant doctrine it may be that; but it may also be an attack on academic integrity, sustained by the university as a whole. It should be the name we give to the intrusion of lock-and-key research into an ostensibly open enterprise." (p. 28)

Costs of Institutional Competition Ineligible for Public Support.

Michael Clurman, "How Shall We Finance Higher Education?" (20004), *The Public Interest,* no. 19 (Spring 70) pp. 98-110. Argues against federal aid to universities based on formulas that would intensify inter-institutional competition, which he holds to be a major cause now contributing to increasing institutional costs per student. Favors instead a price and market system financed through student loans to be repaid from future earnings.

Academic Responsibility: Freedom's Precondition.

Special Committee on Academic Freedom, Responsibility, and Tenure, American Association of State Colleges and Universities, "Statements on Academic Freedom and Responsibility and Academic Tenure" (20005), *Chronicle of Higher Education* (15 Nov 71), p.6. "Academic freedom is the right of members of the academic community freely to study, discuss, investigate, teach, conduct research, publish, or administer, as appropriate to their respective roles and responsibilities. It is the responsibility of administrators to protect and assure these rights within the governing framework of the institution." The statement enumerates a number of responsibilities upon which academic freedom is considered to depend, and restricts the claims of academic freedom to teaching and research within each scholar's professional field.

Proposals for Use of Federal Funds.
U.S Dept. of Health, Education, and Welfare, Assistant Secretary for Planning and Evaluation, "Toward a Long-Range Plan for Federal Financial Support for Higher Education; A Report to the President" (20006), Jan 69. Recommended adding over $7 billion per year by 1976 to existing federal programs assisting higher education, of which the major portion would be an expansion of federal grants for needy and lower middle-income students, also "A program of grants to institutions for planning and evaluation of functions and operations of the institution to improve the efficiency of resource utilization."

Effects of Federal Funding Changes on Academic Science.
National Science Foundation, *Impact of Changes in Federal Science Funding* patterns on Academic Institutions 1968-70 (20007) 82 pp. (Washington: U.S. Government Printing Office, 1970), $0.75. The surveys sampled major research universities and other institutions of higher education (excluding medical schools) awarding doctorates in the science, at both the departmental and institutional level. Crippling adverse impacts of funding reductions were not identified. Expenditures from all sources grew by 7 and 8.5 percent in Fiscal Years 1969 and 1970, respectively, while expenditures of federal funds increased by only 2.4 percent each year. Postdoctoral and faculty appointments grew by 7 and 4 percent, graduate student enrollments stayed constant (although one-third of reporting departments planned to reduce the size of their programs), and department chairman indicated in general that the division of available research funds between senior and young investigators was adequate.

Museums: Institutional System Underlying Descriptive Natural Science.
"The Systematic Biology Collections of the United States; An Essential Resource" (20008) Jan 71, 52 pp. Available from Dr. William C. Steere, President, The New York Botanical Garden, Bronx, New York 10458. A Report to the National Science Foundation by the Conference of Directors of Systematic Collections. Part I, "The Great Collections: Their Nature, Importance, Condition, and Future," identifies the 20 major institutions, which profess their willingness to join in a single national network and coordinate their efforts in order to qualify for increased federal support. Part II is entitled "The Great Collections: Statistical Information."

Symposium on Natural History Collections.
Daniel M. Cohen, ed., "Natural History Collections: Past, Present, and Future" (20009), *Proceedings of the Biological Society of Washington, Vol. 82 [17 Nov 69],* pp. 559-762. Available from the Society, National Museum of Natural History, Smithsonian Institution, Washington, D.C. 20560.

History of Research Museums.
P.J.P. Whitehead, "Museums in the History of Zoology" (20010), *Museums Journal,* Vol. 70, No. 2 (Sep 70), pp. 50-57; and No. 4 (March 71), pp. 155-60.

Universities in Process of Change.
John Caffrey, ed., *The Future Academic Community and Change* (20011) Proceedings of the Annual Meeting of the American Council on Education, October 1968. Available from the Council at 1 Dupont Circle N.W., Washington, D.C. 20036. $7.00.

Diversifying the Degree Structure.
Stephen H. Spurr, for the Carnegie Commission on Higher Education, *Academic Degree Structures: Innovative Approaches* (20012) (New York: McGraw-Hill, 1970) 190 pp. + references, $5.95. Stephen Spurr analyzes the developments in the American academic degree structure and attempts to generalize actual curriculum requirements for basic liberal arts associate's, bachelor's, master's, graduate intermediate, doctor's, and post doctoral degrees—these being the generic names he suggests for each level of study. He suggests that the present system of three levels—bachelor's, master's, and doctor's—is not sufficient to deal with current higher education complexities. Therefore we should introduce into the structure the associate's stage in undergraduate education, a comparable intermediate level in the doctoral program marking the completion of the general studies phase of graduate education, and the postdoctoral stage of scholarly recognition. Students would pass through each level in turn, with the completion of a level carrying no implications as to what a student might elect to do in the following stage. No level would be categorized as terminal or intermediate. "A selection of noninvidious progressive choices should be available to the student at each recognition gate." The author is President of the University of Texas.

International Cooperation in Science.
"Some Thoughts on the National Academy of Sciences and the Role of Nongovernmental Institutions" (20013), *Congressional Record,* 20 May 71, pp. E4751-53. Institutional aspects of international cooperation in science and technology as seen by the Foreign Secretary of the National Academy of Sciences.

The International Meta-University.
Chania, Crete. (20014) prospectus, 8 pp. An international collaborative of scientists, engineers, scholars, and men of affairs whose purpose is to find new ways of meeting the needs of the third world through science and technology. "The program stems from the philosophy that man alone can shape his future if given the opportunity for analysis and the time and the space needed for altruistic planning." Prospectus, published by the International Science Foundation, founded in 1967 by Epimenides Haidemenakis. Noted in *Chemical and Engineering News,* 19 Apr 71, p. 50. Trustees include Dr. Frederick Seitz, President of the Rockefeller University, and Dr. G. H. Stever, then President, Carnegie-Mellon University. Address: 2 rue de Furstenberg, Paris VI.

A New Multi-National Institution for Social Studies.
The European Coordination Centre for Research and Documentation in the Social

Sciences, located in Vienna, will be devoted to interdisciplinary studies of human behavior in the technological society. Described in the *Center Report* (Jun 71), Center for the Study of Democratic Institutions, p. 10. (20015)

Institutional Climate and Creativity.
Donald C. Pelz and Frank M. Andrews, *Scientists in Organizations: Productive Climates for Research and Development* (20016) (New York: John Wiley & Sons, 1966) 260 pp. + appendices, $10.00. The authors gathered extensive data on which to base this study of the relationship between a scientist's performance and the organization of his laboratory, in an attempt to determine what constitutes a stimulating environment for research personnel. The authors considered such factors as freedom, communication with colleagues, work diversification, motivation and dedication, creative ability, and age in collecting information from 1,300 scientists and engineers in basic and applied laboratories, industry, government, and the university. These factors operate jointly as the institutional setting, which may greatly influence the character of research and the likelihood of success. The authors are with the Survey Research Center at the University of Michigan.

Systems Aspects of the Educational Institution Complex.
Michael Marien, "Notes on the Education Complex as an Emerging Macro-System" (20017), in E. O. Attinger, ed., *Global Systems Dynamics* (Basel: Karger, 1970), pp. 225-244.

Institutional Impact of Government-Sponsored Research.
John T. Wilson, "A Dilemma of American Science and Higher Educational Policy: the Support of Individuals and Fields versus the Support of Universities" (20018), *Minerva,* Vol. 9 (Apr 71), pp. 171-96. The research efforts of universities have been unbalanced and their corporate integrity injured by the system of agency support of academic science. A coherent national science policy would take into account the diversity of institutions, as to both type and quality, would vest discretion in creative individuals, and would provide a framework of organization conducive to coherent judgment on the part of Congressional and Executive Branch decision-makers. The author was for many years a leading official of the National Science Foundation and now serves as Provost of the University of Chicago.

Human Values and Higher Education.
Harold C. Lyon, Jr., *Learning to Feel—Feeling to Learn: Humanistic Education for the Whole Man* (20019) (Columbus, Ohio: Charles P. Merrill, 1971) xxii + 321 pp. inc. bibliog., cloth, $7.95; paper, $3.95. Regards the expression of personal experience and feeling as a necessary complement to the intellectual responses that tend to be considered "institutionally correct." Chapters on training, management, and evaluation of "humanistic" educators and processes. Represents in part the practices of the School of Education of the University of Massachusetts, where this book was written. Mr. Lyon serves as Acting Associate Commission of Education for Libraries and Educational Technology.

National Foundation for Higher Education.
Statement by Elliott L. Richardson, Secretary, U.S. Department of Health, Education, and Welfare, before the Subcommittee on Education, Committee on Labor and Public Welfare, U.S. Senate (4 March 71) 13 pp. and handout, 7 pp., U.S. Department of Health, Education, and Welfare (Feb 71)(20020). Plan of organization and summary of proposed legislation offered by Clark Kerr, *Change,* Vol.3, no.3 (May-June 71), p.8 ff.

Woodrow Wilson National Fellowship Foundation.
Suspension of awards, as discussed by the *New York Times* and Dr. Hans Rosenhaupt, Director, entered into the *Congressional Record* for 26 Jan 72, E530-1, by Congressman Halpern of New York. (20021)

Commercial Placement Services.
Council of Better Business Bureaus, Inc., 230 Park Avenue, New York, New York 10017. *Executive Search; Who Does What? A Guide for Job Hunters and Management,* pamphlet, 1971 (20022). Explains the differences among management consultants, executive search firms, public accounting firms, executive clearinghouses, career counselors, and employment agencies.

Investments and the Social Impact of Universities.
John G. Simon, Charles W. Powers, and John P. Gunneman, *The Ethical Investor; Universities and Corporate Responsibility* (20023) (Yale University Press, 1972) x + 208 pp., $9.50 cloth, $2.95 paper. Includes "Suggested Guidelines for the Consideration of Factors Other than Maximum Return in the Management of the University's Investments."

Finances: the Major Pressure for Change.
William G. Bowen, for the Carnegie Commission on Higher Education, 1947 Center Street, Berkeley, California 94704, *The Economics of the Major Private Universities* (20024), 66 pp., $1.25.

Cultural Mission of the University.
F. R. Leavis, *English Literature in Our Time & the University* (20025) (London: Chatto & Windus, 1969) vii + 200 pp., $4.50. Dr. Leavis finds the university the only institution capable of educating the audiences which literature and the arts must have in order to nourish civilization. He argues against direct university patronage of the arts and other creative faculties, fearing that universities will be tempted to divert resources from education and seek to become second-rate impresarios. A provocative application of the concept of an institutional system wherein different goals are seen to be competitive because resources are limited.

The Self-Centered Literature of Higher Education.
Paul L. Dressel and Sally B. Platt, *The World of Higher Education; An Annotated*

Guide to the Major Literature (20026) (San Francisco: Jossey-Bass, 1971), xv + 238 pp. Apart from consideration of federal support, this compendium omits consideration of the cultural, technological, and scientific roles of colleges and universities. It claims to afford staff members engaged in "institutional research" a guide to higher education literature of relevance to them, but also testifies to the narrowness with which issues in higher education have conventionally been drawn.

Shaping an Institution; Roles of Staff and Management.

Ann Mozley, "Change in Argonne National Laboratory: A Case Study; The Impact of Altered Management and Objectives Transform an AEC National Laboratory" (20027), *Science,* Vol. 173 (1 Oct 71), pp. 30-38. Argonne exemplifies the potential for conflict between the breadth that research objectives must have in order to sustain the vigor of staff effort and the narrower focus imposed by agency managers constrained by shrinking budgets. A "concentration policy . . . has brought a shift away from individual and small-group organized work toward the formation of larger complexes for the prosecution of defined research work." In the biological and medical research division of the Laboratory, "once organized substantially on a basis of small groups and individual 'scientific excellence,' researchers have been rearranged around seven major research categories aimed to reflect the overall division mission of the AEC. While this has benefited some division members who now have additional assistants for their research, it has forced other senior and associate biologists into lines divorced from their original research concerns." (p. 35)

Military Contract Research Centers Cut Back.

Nicholas Wade, "Thumbs Down on Think Tanks" (20028), *Science,* Vol. 174 (3 Dec 71), p. 1008. In the judgment of the military appropriations subcommittees of the Congress, the analytic institutions supported by defense contracts to frame plans, policies, and strategies for the armed services are not properly accountable for the effects of their work and have failed to involve the officials properly responsible for national security. The Department of Defense has been instructed to phase out its support of the RAND Corporation (serving the Air Force), the Research Analysis Corporation (serving the Army), the Center for Naval Analysis (Navy), and Institute for Defense Analyses (serving the Department of Defense). Appropriations for this purpose in Fiscal Year 1972 were cut back by one-quarter, "based on giving the Department an opportunity for an orderly phase-down," in the words of the committee report on the House bill.

Finance: A Primary Determinant of Change

Ernest Holsendolph, "A Tale of Two Universities" (20029), *Fortune,* Feb 71, p. 104ff. Praises the University of Southern California for giving up frills and staying solvent, and criticizes Yale for its amentities and institutional style, although giving considerable credit to Yale's managers for their many-sided efforts to overcome deficits. The article shows how financial considerations can affect, and inadvertantly govern, almost every aspect of the life of an institution.

Universities Adrift.
Irving Kristol, "A Different Way to Restructure the University" (20030), *The New York Times Magazine,* 8 Dec 68, p. 50ff. "The real problem at the moment is that no one—not the faculty, not the administration, not the students—has any kind of clear idea of what any 'institution of learning' is supposed to be accomplishing." (p. 176). Kristol's recommendation is to redirect federal aid to students (as was done, to some extent, in the Higher Education Amendments of 1972) in an attempt to increase their involvement in their own education and move toward regenerative pluralism in the institutional system of higher education.

Institutional Change in Research Establishments.
David Fishlock, ed., "Science and Engineering Policy Series," *The New Scientists* (20031) (Oxford University Press, 1971) 98 pp., $3.00. Of the six expert essays on research management in Britain collected in this volume, two deal with the critical topic of institutional receptivity to change. Hans Kronberger's essay relates how a sense of purpose was created and program effectiveness maintained in the Risley research establishment of the British Atomic Energy Authority, not in spite of but largely because demanding tasks succeeded one another at a challenging pace. In "Harwell Changes Course," W. Marshall, the youthful Director of the Atomic Energy Research Establishment, outlines thirteen specific and four general problems that had to be addressed in redeploying its scientific resources. Institutional inertia turned out to be a non-problem. "A large number (of staff scientists) welcomed the opportunity to do something exciting and new. Industrial research, it turns out, is as great a challenge intellectually as atomic energy research." (p. 62) The real and difficult problems lay in institutional integration with industry. His account of how they were overcome may be read with profit by anyone seeking to change the external orientation of a research establishment.

Bibliography on Improvement of Undergraduate Education.
Paul G. Tamminen, "A Guide to Resources for Undergraduate Academic Reform" (20032) American Council on Education, "Special Report," 30 June 70, 15 pp.

Institutional Alternatives to Academic Science.
Harold Orlans, for the Carnegie Commission on Higher Education, *The Nonprofit Research Institute: Its Origin, Operation, Problems and Prospects* (20033) (N.Y.: McGraw-Hill, 1972), 180 pp., bibliog., $6.95. Reviewed in PROMETHEUS One/four by Rodney Nichols, pp. 141-145.

Nonprofit Institutions in Science.

National Science Foundation, "Surveys of Science Resources," NSF 71-9, *Scientific Activities of Independent Nonprofit Institutions 1970* (20034) (Washington: U.S. Government Printing Office, 1971) x, 63 pp., $0.70. Of 426 responding institutions, 159 are classified as research institutes (employing 10,105 scientists and engineers, not all full-time), 27 federally funded research and development centers administered by nonprofit institutions (employing 6,057 scientists and engineers), 147 voluntary hospitals (employing 4,331 scientists and engineers), and 93 other nonprofit organizations (employing 3,159 scientists and engineers).

Summary of Data

	Research Institutes	FFRDC's	Voluntary Hospitals	Other Orgnztns
Source of Funds for R&D				
Federal Government	224,379	262,564	84,228	35,424
State government	7,265	477	1,723	1,330
Local government	2,430	2,912	193	524
Foundations	12,744	1,423	9,069	5,195
Voluntary health agencies	4,255	—	3,890	152
Industry	73,566	3,419	1,773	2,514
Institution's own funds	25,904	5,003	24,222	26,355
Other	10,476	1,516	5,148	5,226
Research Expenditures for 1969				
Engineering	113,648	138,459	153	5,437
Physical sciences	47,990	46,561	2,137	7,055
Environmental sciences	8,293	5,045	79	3,353
Mathematics	14,252	20,195	738	216
Life sciences	101,073	14,073	123,166	27,655
Psychology	14,741	5,717	3,192	6,193
Social sciences	53,724	32,049	415	13,743
Other sciences	7,298	15,215	366	13,068

State Governments.

National Science Foundation, "Surveys of Science Resources," NSF 70-22, *Research and Development in State Government Agencies; Fiscal Years 1967 & 1968* (20035) (Washington: U.S. Government Printing Office, 1970) xi, 93 pp., $1.00. State government agencies spent $131 million for R&D in fiscal year 1968, half derived from the Federal Government. The largest fields were health and hospitals (43%), natural resources (25%), highways (13%), and education (10%). 9,137 persons (full-time equivalent) were employed in R&D, 41% scientists and engineers.

Local Governments.
National Science Foundation, "Surveys of Science Resources," NSF 71-6, *Research and Development in Local Governments; Fiscal Years 1968 & 1969* (20036) (Washington: U.S. Government Printing Office, 1971) x, 55 pp., $0.65. Local government R&D expenditures were $40 million in 1969, double the 1966 level, half derived from the Federal Government. The largest fields were health and hospitals (39%), education (13%), sanitation (12%), and police and corrections (11%). Approximately 2,600 full-time equivalent personnel were employed by local governments in R&D.

Social Problem Solving and the University.
Richard F. Ericson, "Toward Increasing the Social Relevance of the Contemporary University" (20037) , Program of Policy Studies in Science and Technology, The George Washington University, Aug 69, 31 pp. Describes plans for a Comparative Cybernetic Studies Group.

Cutbacks in Industrial Research.
Deborah Shapley, "Industrial Laboratories: Whither Basic Research?" (20038) *Science,* Vol. 174 (17 Dec 71), pp. 1214-15. In recent months four companies heretofore strongly committed to basic research have cut back or discontinued programs.

Congressional Defense of the RAND Corporation.
Congressman Charles H. Wilson, "RAND and Its Work" (20039), *Congressional Record,* 4 Feb 72, E844-45. Contends that RAND and its analytic capabilities are badly needed in order to address social problems.

Institutional Factors and Industrial Research Productivity.
Donald W. Collier, "An Innovation System for the Larger Company" (20040), 29 Dec. 69, 8 pp. Recommends means of operating an industrial research laboratory in a large company-while retaining the productivity that often characterizes only smaller firms.

Educational Research: The Quagmire Deepens.
Roger F. Levien, *National Institute of Education: Preliminary Plan for the Proposed Institute* (20041) (Santa Monica, Calif.: RAND Corporation, (1971), Report 657-HEW, xvii, 199 pp. While confessing that the problems to be addressed by educational research are not yet determined (!), this report lays out a plan for a new education research agency with a starting budget of $130 million to grow by an additional billion over ten years. One rationale offered is that no more than one-fourth as many dollars are spent for research and development in education as in agriculture, while the two fields were comparable at 5 and 7 percent of GNP respectively. Consider this statement: "Illumination of the nature of education's crucial problems would be a major function of the NIE: the intramural

R&D activity would play a central role in this process. However, that illumination has not yet been performed, so an adequate definition of problems warranting national R&D efforts does not exist." (p.viii) The proposed Institute would administer training programs and other projects devoted to "moving the state of the art forward" at all levels of education, preschool to doctoral. Three-quarters of the Institute's resources should be devoted to problem-oriented research and development and the advancement of educational practice. The remaining resources would be for the support of studies in adjacent disciplines such as psychology or educational media and for a program of intramural research. Also the text of S.434, A Bill to Establish a National Institute of Education (29 Jan 71) 8 pp.; Statement by Secretary Elliott Richardson to the Select Committee on Education of the U.S. House of Representatives (17 March 71) 8 pp.; Statement by Commissioner of Education Sidney P. Marland, Jr., to the same committee (17 March 71) 9 pp.; and Statement by Don Davies, Acting Deputy Commissioner for Development to the same committee (14 May 71) 3 pp.

Interdisciplinary Studies Committee on the Future of Man.
V.R. Potter *et al.,* "Purpose and Function of the University" (20042), *Science,* Vol. 167 (20 Mar 70), pp. 1590-93. Describes new program at the University of Wisconsin at Madison.

University as a Source of Social Regeneration.
Peter Schrag, "New Beat in the Heart of Dixie" (20043), *Saturday Review* (20 Mar 71), p. 42 ff. Institutional profile of the University of Alabama. Having missed out on funds for major research and failed to achieve academic distinction of the conventional kind, the University of Alabama may help the South to serve as "a reservoir for renewal and re-creation" for the Nation.

Universities and the Urban Poor.
Organization for Social and Technical Innovation (20044),, U.S. Office of Education 50062, *Urban Universities: Rhetoric, Reality, and Conflict* (Washington: U.S. Government Printing Office, June 70), vi, 65 pp., $0.65. Emphasizes barriers to communication and coincidence of view between universities and the urban poor.

Educational Research.
A Review of Research and Development Centers Supported by the U.S. Office of Education (20045),, reprinted from *The Journal of Research and Development in Education* (summer, 1968). OE 12040 (Washington: U.S. Government Printing Office, 1969) 202 pp. Program descriptions and lists of publications for nine federally funded centers for educational research and development.

Institutions for Human Purpose.
Phillip J. Gallagher and George D. Demos, *The Counseling Center in Higher Education* (20046) (Springfield, I.: Charles C. Thomas, 1970) xiv + 399 pp., $13.75. This informative compilation describes various aspects and functions of counseling centers in colleges and universities. Most such centers at larger universities combine educational, occupational, and personal counseling. (p. 37) David Palmer, Associate Dean of Counseling, University of California at Los Angeles, describes the UCLA counseling services program, which has responded sensitively to the concerns of today's students. For a start, no records are kept. "This policy is a thing of the spirt, though held by many to be a quixotic practice. Quixote, however, was a champion of the spirit, and such qualities may have critical importance in an eroding, material world—especially in services which seek to deal with the spirit." (p. 291) Every student is seen at once, even if only for a brief orientation interview. Staff members are gently discouraged from adopting the self-image of the research-oriented psychologist; many prepared in other fields of study. "A community is being served and the needs served are many: the models and insights of one discipline are insufficient. The ultimate understandings sought are of man, his existence, his stages of growth." (p. 298) The waiting room is physically attractive, with exhibits prepared by staff members who have taught or served in other countries. "Each is evidence of man's diversity and his richness, his customs and his intimations of understanding." Instead of magazines there are children's books on the tables. "Children's books were deliberately chosen, first, because they are frequently the best flowerings of the combined arts of the illustrator, writer, and printer. Second, because, like Ets' little *Come Play with Me*, they are frequently eloquent presentations of profound truths. They touch students often through the aesthetic and affective modes of recognition which our university culture so frequently neglects and which are so essential to the individual." (p. 306) If an institution had a heart one hopes it would be like that. Bravo, David Palmer!

Political Pressures and Institutions of Higher Education.
Sheldon S. Wolin and John H. Schaar, *The Berkeley Rebellion and Beyond; Essays on Politics & Education in the Technological Society* (20047) (N.Y.: New York Review of Books, 1970), 158 pp. $1.95. Two former members of the Berkeley political science faculty analyze the conflicting political forces at play within and upon contemporary universities.

A Document on the Hollowness of Higher Education.
James Simon Kunen, *The Strawberry Statement—Notes of a College Revolutionary* (20048) (N.Y.: Random House, 1969) 151 pp., $4.95. One can gain a vivid impression of the weakness and emptiness of Columbia University, its systematic failure to comprehend its institutional situation, which brought on the destructive

upheavals of 1968, from this little essay, although its student-author offers little more than a hasty sketch of his own impressions and actions.

Legal Aspects of Student-Institutional Relationships.
Otis A. Singletary and Robert B. Yegge, consultant-editors, *Denver Law Journal,* Vol. 45, no. 4, special issue, 1968, pp. 497-678. (20049)

Consortium of Five Massachusetts Colleges.
Amherst, Hampshire, Mount Holyoke, and Smith Colleges and the University of Massachusetts, *Five College Cooperation: Directions for the Future,* Report of the Five College Long-Range Planning Committee, 1969, 228 pp. Available from the University of Massachusetts Press, Amherst, Massachusetts 01002, $5.00. Deals with academic complementarity, cooperative academic programs, student course exchange, four-one-four calendar, supplementary academic activities, coeducation and cooperation, student life, cooperative planning and use of facilities and services, and economic consequences of cooperation. (2.01002)

Institutional Self-Study: Faculty Government.
Harvard University, "Preamble and Procedures" Committee on Rights and Responsibilities, Faculty of Arts and Sciences, 16 Feb 71, 48 pp. incl. first draft and amendments. Details complaint and hearing procedures to protect the mutual obligations of members of the university community. Based on a resolution of the Faculty of Arts and Sciences which recognized "the responsibility of officers of administration and instruction to be alert to the needs of the University community; to give full and fair hearing to reasoned expressions of grievances; and to respond promptly and in good faith to such expressions and to widely-expressed needs for change." (2.02138)

Institutional Self-Study: Graduate School.
Harvard University, "Report of the Committee on the Future of the Graduate School" Mar 69, 38 pp. Recommends a reduction in the size of the Graduate School, a Graduate Student Center, and several provisions "for enabling graduate students to become part of the scholarly world as early as possible." Members of the Committee are Herschel C. Baker, William N. Lipscomb, Robert G. McCloskey, Robert W. White, and Robert Lee Wolff, Chairman. (2.02138)

Institutional Self-Study: Faculty Organization.
Harvard University, *"Report of the Committee on the Organization of the Faculty of Arts and Sciences"* 17 Oct 69, 31 pp. Recommends a Faculty Council, joint student-faculty committees on undergraduate and graduate education and student and community relations. Members: Harry T. Levin, Konrad Bloch, Giles Constable, Andrew M. Gleason, Don K. Price, Howard Berg, Kenneth M. Deitch, James C. Thomson, Jr. (2.02138)

Academic Tenure.

University Committee on Governance, Harvard University, *Discussion Memorandum on Academic Tenure at Harvard University,* Nov 71, 40 pp. (2.02138).

Institutional Self-Study: Financial Structure.

Harvard University Committee on Governance, "Harvard and Money: A Memorandum in Issues and Choices" Nov 70, 19 pp. A frank and even witty analysis of financial questions whose influence on institutions has perhaps nowhere been sufficiently understood. "Since the early 19th century, and certainly since the presidency of Mr. Conant, the University has operated on the principle that, over time, each 'unit' should by and large finance itself. 'Every tub on its own bottom' (ETOB), though not enforced with uniform strategy, has dominated the allocation of financial resources. The governing strategy for raising new resources, it has powerfully affected the University's shape. . . . Financially, Harvard is a confederation of baronies, squirearchies, and small farms. . . . The amount of discretion available to the center in the allocation of money has been exceedingly limited. It is fair to say that the present shape of Harvard reflects some 300 years' worth of bargains between generations of presidents, deans, professors, and administrators, on the one hand, and donors on the other." (pp. 6-8) The University, as distinguished from its ten schools, administers no government contracts and had a total income of $7.9 million out of a total of $176.3 million during 1968-69. (2.02138)

Institutional Consideration of Its Raison d'Etre.

Harvard University Committee on Governance, "The Nature and Purposes of the University; A Discussion Memorandum, Interim Report" Jan 71, 9 pp. "In many quarters today the ideal of an institution devoted to the search for truth by open inquiry has lost credibility. Why?

"Has this ideal lost credibility within the university because too many university men have been diverted from the search for truth? To be blunt—the answer is yes. To put it more judiciously, we need to ask ourselves some difficult questions." (p. 3)

"In the last analysis all individual and institutional commitment to a search for truth through the process of reason has rested on faith—upon the belief that man is a rational and social being endowed with a sense of justice that enables him to choose between good and evil; that he must choose for himself; that there are circumstances that best facilitate that choice; and that we must do what we can to bring this to pass. This traditional faith is less easily defended now than fifty years ago. For one thing, we have learned that reasoning is a less simple process than was once supposed. We are more mindful of the darker, frightening side of man. On the brighter side, we are more ready to agree that spontaneity, intuition, love—all the life of feeling that we associated with the ways of the poet and the artist—may save the processes of the intellect from sterility and desiccation. The insight of the social sciences and the honesty of the arts have taught us to look at ourselves stripped of pretense and what we see is less than lovely. It takes honesty and courage to see ourselves as we are; but perhaps we should strive to regain the greater Hellenic courage to see man stumble and fall, yet avow his nobler capacity." (pp. 6-7) (2.02138)

Roles and Responsibilities in Governance.
Harvard University Committee on Governance, *The Organization and Functions of the Governing Boards and the President's Office; A Discussion Memorandum* (2.02138) (March 71) 40 pp. The memorandum affirms the trust responsibilities of governing boards on behalf of "the public which even for a private university determines its objectives." Implicit throughout the report is a finding that too much time of the Corporation, president, and financial staff is devoted to routine detail and that overall institutional planning, especially its educational dimension, has suffered as a result.

Institutional Self-Study: Faculty Government.
Harvard University Committee on Governance, "Tentative Recommendations Concerning Discipline of Officers" Mar 71, 9 pp. Violations of the University-wide Statement on Rights and Responsibilities (defining essential freedoms in the community) or the university statute on tenure which makes officers of instruction subject to removal "only for grave misconduct or neglect of duty" are to be investigated by a Screening Committee of the faculty concerned, and then made subject to the recommendations of a Hearing Committee drawn from that faculty in part, with a majority composed of members of other faculties of the university. (2.02138)

Institutional Self-Study: Rights and Responsibilities.
Harvard University Committee on Governance, "Tentative Recommendations Concerning Rights and Responsibilities" Apr 70, 15 pp. Reports cited available from the Committee, Wadsworth House, Cambridge, Mass. 02138. Proposes university-wide adoption of the procedures originated by the Committee on Rights and Responsibilities of the Faculty of Arts and Sciences. Chairman of the Committee on Governance is John T. Dunlop. (2.02138)

Off-Campus Study—Abroad.
Educational Expeditions International. 21 pp. program announcement available on request; P.O. Box 127, Belmont, Mass. 02178. A nonprofit educational service arranging for students to participate in scientific expeditions overseas. Preliminary prospectus for an archaeological expedition to Zambia, a geologic field survey in Ecuador, a volcano survey in Costa Rica, a meteorite search in South West Africa, and an exploratory expedition to a little-known mountain range in Ethiopia. (2.02178)

Youth in Service: The Dartmouth Experience.
Dartmouth College. (2.03755). Documents include "A Handbook for the New

Hampshire General Court" Jan 71, 37 pp., a manual for state legislators prepared by student interns; annual report, "Office of Regional Programs" 28 Feb 71, 11 pp., eight documents on the William Jewett Tucker Foundation, a special agency to fund off-campus learning, including "Conscience and the Undergraduate" by John Sloan Dickey, Apr 55, and "A Better Chance," describing student teaching in underprivileged school systems, 46 pp.

Governance and the Concept of Community.
President's Commission on the Organization of the Faculty, Dartmouth College. Summary statement (2.03755)(6 April 71) 60 pp. Recommends creation of an overall Council with a novel scheme of voting to guarantee representation to determined minorities, as well as faculty reorganization, appointment of a dean of undergraduate studies, and creation of a program of public policy studies.

Institutional Self-Study.
University of New Hampshire, *Toward Unity through Diversity*, 15 Feb 67, viii + 100 pp., Report of the University-wide Educational Policies Committee. (2.03824)

Institutional Self-Study: Curriculum.
University of New Hampshire, *The University of New Hampshire and the Future*, Sept 60, 117 pp. Report of the Committee on Academic Programs and Teaching Methods. (2.03824)

The Academic Register. (2.06470)
The Education Exchange, Box 392, Newtown, Conn. 06470, *The Academic Register*. Publishes concise resumes of candidates for positions in colleges, junior colleges, public schools in any of three regions, private schools, and overseas: one-time filing fee of $15.00 for publication in each.

Proposals on Role of Alumni.
Yale University, *Report on the Commission of Alumni Affairs* Dec 70, vii + 117 pp. Available from the Office of the Secretary of the University, Woodbridge Hall, New Haven, Conn. 06520. A wide-ranging review of alumni relations, with a number of noteworthy proposals, including a recommendation that two students or junior faculty members be assigned as research assistants to each trustee. (2.06520)

Calendar Change to Accommodate Curriculum Reform.
Marvin Bressler, "A Report to the Commission on the Future of the College for Discussion by the Princeton University Community" (2.08540), 86 pp.

College Board Review.
(2.08540) Quarterly publication of the College Entrance Examination Board.

David Coleman, Editor, 888 Seventh Avenue, New York, N.Y. 10019. Subscriptions, $2.00 per year, from Box 592, Princeton, N.J. 08540.

Educational Career Service.
12 Nassau Street, Princeton, N.J. 08540. Nonprofit membership placement service for academic and administrative positions, some programs conducted in cooperation with educational associations.

Bulletin on Employment Opportunities.
Modern Language Association in cooperation with the Association of Departments of English and the Association of Departments of Foreign Languages, *Job Information List*, subscription rate $10.00 per year for members, $15.00 for nonmembers. In October, December, February, and May publishes concise statements about departmental hiring plans for the forthcoming academic year. Many departments, having filled their positions, notify candidates not to write, and are thereby freed of the need to acknowledge the receipt of form letters. Some representative entries: "Concerning the three positions mentioned in earlier Job Information Lists: we now have all the letters of application we will be able to consider. . ."; "No vacancies anticipated for 1972. Please do not write"; "Four positions now open. If you applied earlier and are still available, please notify us that you wish your application to be active. Applicants will be considered only in the designated areas of . . ."; "The previously listed position has been filled." A worthy experiment and distinctive service. One wonders if it could be broadened into fields such as publishing, editing, and library service. (2.10002)

A Prescription for Continuous Institutional Renewal.
New York University, *The Report of the Commission on Undergraduate Education* (2.10003)(13 May 1971) 137 pp. Recommends the creation of an Office of Academic Development to incorporate institutional research, combined with twenty student internships to support continuous study and reappraisal of the university's educational offerings.

Commission on Non-Traditional Study.
A review of credit and credentials in higher education, created by the College Entrance Examination Board and the Educational Testing Service, 888 Seventh Avenue, New York, New York 10019. Description of its program by John A. Valentine, Executive Secretary, in PROMETHEUS One/two, pp. 35-38. (2.10019)

Education and World Affairs.
522 Fifth Ave., New York, New York 10036. "To assist in strengthening the performance of American higher educational institutions in world affairs in all its principal dimensions—teaching of Americans, conduct of research, exchange of persons, and cooperation with educational institutions and efforts abroad." (2.10036)

DIRCO.
Peter J. Dirr, President, P.O. Box 17, Elnora, New York 12065. DIRCO is a year-old educational corporation established to provide tailored consultation services to educational institutions. The Open University Consultant Team is a group of individuals, all of whom have backgrounds in curriculum design, cooperative education, educational broadcasting, information storage/retrieval, independent study, and research and evaluation. The composition of the team may vary depending upon the needs of the contracting institution. (2.12065)

Planned Change through Reshaping Physical Plant.
Doxiadis Associates, Inc., *Campus Planning in an Urban Area; A Master Plan for Rensselaer Polytechnic Institute* (2.12181) (N.Y.: Praeger, "Praeger Special Studies in U.S. Economic and Social Development," 1971), 99 pp. + 25 maps.

State University of New York.
"The Master Plan, Revised, 1968" *Creation of the Future: Priorities of Growth and Change* (2.12201) 45 pp. and supplement.

Notes on the Future of Education.
Quarterly publication(2.13210) of the Educational Policy Research Center, 1206 Harrison Street, Syracuse, New York 13210. D.J. Barclay, editor.

The College Placement Council, Inc.
65 East Elizabeth Avenue, P. O. Box 2263, Bethlehem, Pennsylvania 18001. Maintains a library on career counseling, placement, and recruitment in higher education; represents placement and recruitment interests of about 1,200 colleges and universities and 2,000 employers. Executive Director: Robert F. Herrick. (2.18001)

Defining the Objectives of a Small Liberal Arts College.
Cedar Crest College, Allentown, Pennsylvania 18104, A Three Year Profile 1967/1970, 24 pp. (2.18104)

National Student Lobby.
(2.20003) 413 East Capitol Street, Washington, D.C., 20003. Story by Eric Wentworth of the *Washington, Post,* entered into the *Congressional Record* by Senator Fred Harris, 11 Apr 72, S5833. Other documents and reports.

dta Reports.
Douglas Trout Associates, 888 17th Street, N.W., Washington, D.C. 20006. Newsletter at intervals for clients of higher education consulting firm specializing in problems of the small college. (2.20006)

Curriculum Advisory Service.
The Consultants' Bureau, Office of Biological Education, American Institute of Biological Sciences, 3900 Wisconsin Avenue, N.W., Washington, D.C. 20016. (2.20016)

Cooperative College Registry.
One Dupont Circle, Washington, D.C. 20036. *A Manual for Member Colleges and Universities,* 23 pp. Originally formed to assist small denominational colleges in attracting candidates for faculty positions, recently broadened to all colleges. Candidates file a one-page personal abstract (no fee). Institutions pay one-time search fees or sustaining membership fees. In January, 1971 there were 3,742 candidates in the files. Executive Director: Mrs. Elizabeth S. Fisher.   (2.20036)

National Board on Graduate Education.
National Research Council, 2101 Constitution Avenue, N.W., Washington, D.C. 20418. "New graduate programs must be devised in response to the changing body of knowledge and to our need for persons educated to cope with urgent, newly emerging problems. These matters deserve the concentrated attention of graduate schools, employers, and governmental and private organizations concerned with graduate education." Quotation from a conference on predoctoral education in 1969, leading to establishment of a 25-member Board by the Conference Board of Associated Research Councils to undertake "an unbiased, thorough analysis of graduate education today and of its relation to American society in the future." Program leaflet (2.20418).

Board on Human Resources. (2.20418)
A Board on Human Resources has been established by the National Research Council to make a broad survey of national education and manpower problems and select specific areas for in-depth study. The group will consider a wide range of studies, including an evaluation of social and economic returns on higher education and an analysis of the vast education and manpower data-collection systems. In addition to conducting some studies itself, the board will stimulate studies by other groups. The Russell Sage Foundation has pledged $50,000 a year for five years as partial support for the board. Further financial support is being sought from other sources. Ten members representing the social and natural sciences have been appointed to the board by Philip Handler, President of the National Academy of Sciences. The chairman is Robert W. Morse, former President of Case Western Reserve University. The NRC's Office of Scientific Personnel will provide staff services.
     "Human resources" has become a popular term for describing the complex question of how the nation can best develop the personal talents of its citizens for the benefit of the individual and the good of society. In recent years of burgeoning college enrollments, campus dissent about the quality of education, fluctuating financial support for education and research, and a growing need for skilled personnel to deal with social problems, attention has been focused on training and utilization of specialized manpower. Therefore, the new Human Resource Board expects to give early consideration to such questions of higher education as: How do the American society and economy benefit from the increasingly more costly investment in higher education? Is a national wave of "cre-

dentialitis" creating an artificial demand for undergraduate and graduate degrees? Is formal education really necessary to provide manpower for many jobs that now require college degrees? Are the beneficiaries of education—the individual, the employer, and society—sharing fairly in education costs? The board, however, will not restrict itself to formal education and the white-collar worker. Unlike short-lived groups established to produce a single report on a specific topic, the new board hopes to take a larger, and longer, view of the full range of human resources problems. Other possible topics for exploration include the effects of longer life expectancy and earlier retirement on the individual and on manpower utilization; retraining opportunities for persons at all skill levels who are forced to or wish to change occupations in mid-career; effects on manpower utilization of changes in government policy, such as reduced defense spending or approval of family-assistance programs; and long-range trends indicated by the wealth of education and employment data collected by government and private agencies.

Other members of the board are: Daniel Bell, Department of Social Relations, Harvard University; Ivan L. Bennett, Jr., Director, New York University Medical Center; William D. Carey, Senior Staff Associate, Arthur D. Little, Inc.; Kenneth E. Clark, Dean, College of Arts and Sciences, University of Rochester; Diana Crane, Department of Behavioral Sciences, The Johns Hopkins University; Edgar G. Epps, Department of Education, University of Chicago; Wayland C. Griffith, Vice President for Research, Research and Development Division, Lockheed Missiles and Space Company, Lockheed Aircraft Corporation; Paul J. Taubman, Associate Professor of Economics, University of Pennsylvania; and Dael Wolfle, Graduate School of Public Affairs, University of Washington.

Under the Chairmanship of Paul Taubman, Professor of Economics, University of Pennsylvania, the Board has established a Panel on the Benefits of Higher Education, whose staff director is Dr. Lewis C. Solmon. The panel will investigate the extent to which monetary returns to education vary with family background, mental ability, and school quality, and also seek to assess the proper role for the Federal Government in funding higher education. The social benefits of higher education will be explored in a future phase of this inquiry.

Institutional Inventory of Study Resources.
Smithsonian Institution, *Smithsonian Opportunities for Research and Study.* Published annually. About 100 pp. incl. index of staff specialties. Available from the Office of Academic Studies, Smithsonian Institution, Washington, D.C. 20560. A unique directory to reinterpret a complex establishment in terms of academic disciplines more familiar to university faculty members than would be its normal table of organization. (2.20560)

Proposal for an Experimental College.
Experimental College Committee, Faculty Senate, University of Maryland, .

"Building a Relevant University" (2.20742), report published in *Argus*, Feb 71, p. 4ff.

Reorientation toward Undergraduate Concerns.
The Johns Hopkins University, Academic Council, Blue Ribbon Committee on Undergraduate Education, Final Report (2.21218). *The Johns Hopkins Gazette,* 9 Mar 72, 4 pp.

Johns Hopkins University.
Long Range Planning Committee, *Report to the President* (June 66), 221 pp. (2.21218)

Managing Change in Purposive Organizations.
Igor Ansoff, "A Strategic Plan for the Graduate School of Management," Vanderbilt University (2.37203), Sept. 68, 43 pp., mimeo.

An Institution under Stress.
Robert W. Morse, documents illustrating the factors which prompted his resignation as President of Case Western Reserve University. (2.44106) Also see "Universities: Dusk or Dawn?" PROMETHEUS One/one, pp. 23-31.

Individual Goals and Organizational Objectives;
A. Study of Integration Mechanisms, by Jon H. Barrett, Center for Research in the Utilization of Scientific Knowledge, Institute for Social Research, University of Michigan, (2.48104) 1970. ix, 119 pp. $3.00. Barrett compared the fulfillment of organizational and individual purpose through a survey of skilled and professional workers in an oil refinery, employing a quantitative index of goal integration based on answers to questions about the extent to which the company satisfied their individual needs and *vice versa.* The greatest effectiveness was found where individual and organizational goals were considered to be reinforcing rather than just compatible. Although objectives are here defined simply as the functions of organizations rather than the purposes distinguishing institutions this study encourages the belief that institutional objectives must be substantially derived from the professional aims of their members.

W. E. Upjohn Institute for Employment Research.
300 South Westnedge Avenue, Kalamazoo, Michigan 49007. "A Twenty-Year Review" (1965), vii + 30 pp. and Publications Order lists. The Institute also maintains a research office in Washington, D.C. (2.49007)

Program for Independent Study.
Ottawa University *The New Plan of Education for Ottawa University* 2nd ed. (Jul 70), vi + 117 pp. + supplements. Also *A Forward Step: Ottawa University's New Program for Individual Development,* (Bulletin, 1970, 32 pp.) Describes individualized advising committees, student contracts for specific graduation

requirements, off-campus experience, core studies, depth studies, electives, and evaluation. (2.66067)

Accounting for the Stability of an Institution.
Deborah Shapley, "Kansas State U.: Whatever Happened to Good Old State U.?" (2.66502), *Science,* 19 Nov 71, pp. 803-5.

Education Commission of the States.
Bulletin; Higher Education in the States (2.80203). 1860 Lincoln Street, Suite 300, Denver, Colorado 80203.

Western Interstate Commission on Higher Education.
(2.80302) Post Office Drawer P, Boulder, Colorado 80302, *Reports on Higher Education,* monthly bulletin. Also annual reports.

Redefining the Liberal Arts College.
Ronald C. Nairn, "A New Enterprise for Education" (2.86301), description by its president of new programs and directions for Prescott College, Prescott, Arizona. 50 pp.

Human Values Ascend.
David Palmer, "What to Expect of Counsel" (2.90024), pamphlet on resources available in the Counseling Center of the University of California, Los Angeles. 12 pp. Also David Palmer, "A Hyphenated Profession" (1972), 33 pp.

Ethnically Oriented College.
Third College Planning Committee, *Third College Academic Plan* University of California, San Diego, 22 pp. (2.92037)

A Major Blueprint for Change.
The Study of Education at Stanford, *Report to the University* (2.94305), ten volumes, 1968.

Reappraisal of the Institutional System of Higher Education.
Carnegie Commission on Higher Education, 1947 Center Street, Berkeley, California 94704. Leaflet and publications list. (2.94704)

Study of University Governance.
University of California, Berkeley, *The Culture of the University: Governance and Education; Report of the Study Commission on University Governance,* 15 Jan 68, 95 pp. + 8 oversize pp. (2.94720) Also a dissenting report, "The Challenge to the University," by Albert Fishlow and David Freedman.

Journal of Educational Change.
(2.94720) Published irregularly by the Office of the Assistant Chancellor for Edu-

cational Development, 200 California Hall, University of California, Berkeley, California 94720, to describe new academic offerings and facilities which the University considers to be responsive to student interests.

University of California, Santa Cruz.
Long Range Development Plan (1963), 44 pp., and *Academic Plan 1965-1975* (1965), 29 pp. (2.95060).

An Educational Commune.
The Learning Community Published by participants in an educational experiment. 15 pp., boxed, with supplements, $3.50 per year; 215 SE Ninth Ave., Portland, Oregon 97214. "We are a learning community, neither a commune nor a college. Experimental colleges will continue to be created by people who feel unable to learn well in conventional institutions, and communes by those who feel unable to live well in conventional social patterns. We want to change our learning and our lives. We want to make a community committed to education, and a place of learning committed to the wholeness of life. We want to make connections between intellect and emotion, study and action, the past and the present, the city and the country, the working life and the personal life, the cooperative group and the general society." (2.97214)

Innovation through the New Institution.
David G. Barry, "Academic Planning in a Time of Change" and other documents on Evergreen State College, Washington. (2.98501)

Restructuring Teacher Education.
Committee on Inquiry under the Chairmanship of Lord James of Rusholme, Department of Education and Science, United Kingdom, *Teacher Education and Training, The Times Higher Education Supplement,* 28 Jan 72, 12 pp. (2.U.K..)

Council for Academic Freedom and Democracy.
(2.U.K.) Reports of investigations, *Newsletter,* and annual reports, available from the Council, 152 Camden High Street, London NW1 ONN, England.

Higher Education Research Unit.
London School of Economics and Political Science, Houghton Street, Aldwych, London WC2A 2AE England. "Reprint Series" and "Books" (2.U.K..).

An Exemplary Self-Study.
University of Oxford, *Report of Commission of Inquiry* (Oxford: Clarendon Press, 1966), two vols., 428 pp. and 496 pp. (2. U.K..)

3. Technology, Communications

Mark Podwal

THE ABM

Civilian Agencies Must Not Abdicate Role in Science.
U.S. Senator Thomas J. McIntyre Statement (3000) calling for technological R&D work by civilian agencies, press release, 24 Feb 71. "Since a strong technological base is essential to our security and internal health as a nation, we must depend on all arms of the government—not just the Pentagon—to accomplish this goal." McIntyre's complete statement was printed in PROMETHEUS One/one; it includes details of his efforts to increase the research budget of the National Science Foundation; similar moves to stimulate research activities by civilian agencies constitute "one way the military R&D budget can be brought into balance."

Documents on Engineering and the Humanities.
David P. Billington, Professor of Civil Engineering, Princeton University, three papers (3001), as follows: "Dean's Page," *The Princeton Engineer,* Feb 70, pp. 7, 18, 20, 22; "An Engineering Program; Engineering and the Humanities," 25 Nov 70, 5 pp.; and "Civil Engineering; History, Heritage and the Humanities," The Princeton University Conference, Meeting No. 103, 14-16 Oct 70, 12 pp.

Businessmen for a Peacetime Economy.
Businessmen's Educational Fund, *Economic Conversion and Business Responsibility* (3002) 16 pp. 515 Madison Avenue, New York, New York 10022.

Domestic Problems and Public Priorities.
Businessmen's Educational Fund, "BEF's First Year, A Report on the Businessmen's Educational Fund" (3003), 1971, 16 pp. Subtitled "When Peace Breaks Out: Economic Conversion and Business Responsibility." The Fund seeks allocations of larger shares of talent and resources to domestic problems.

Reducing the Dependence of Academic Science on Military Patronage.
Senator Tom McIntyre, enactment of substitute amendment to the Military Procurement Appropriation Act. 28 Aug 70, *Congressional Record,* S14551-561. (3004)

Defense Brief for Military Support of Research.
Naval Research Advisory Committee, "Basic Research in the Navy" (3005), 171 pp., charts. 1959. An extensive justification of military support of academic science.

Commentary on Mission-Oriented Research.
U.S House of Representatives, Committee on Science and Astronautics, "Mission Agency Report of Basic Research" (3006), (Mar 70). 5 pp. A report to the Subcommittee on Science, Research, and Development; reprinted in the *Bulletin of the Atomic Scientists* (Sep 70).

Defense of Military Support of Academic Science.
William J. Price, "The Case for Agency Research" (3007), *Bulletin of the Atomic*

Scientists (Apr 69), pp. 34-36. Price was Executive Director of the Air Force's Office of Scientific Research.

Military R&D Falters.
John Walsh, "Project Themis: Budget Cuts, Critics, Cause Phase Out" (3008), *Science*, Vol. 169 (21 Aug 70), p. 749. Demise of a Defense Department R&D funding program intended to stimulate creation of new academic "centers of excellence."

New Left Blamed for Hostility toward Technology.
Lawrence Lessing, "The Senseless War on Science" (3009), *Fortune*, March 71, p. 88ff. Attacks the youth culture for dedication to "astrology, drugs, and those eastern mysticisms that for centuries have held whole continents impoverished." (p. 90)

Human Factors in Performance Standards.
James R. Wright, "Performance Criteria in Building" (3010), *Scientific American*, Vol. 223, No. 3 (Mar 71) pp. 17-25. Describes work by the Educational Facilities Laboratories, Inc., and the National Bureau of Standards on the principle that human requirements should be the basis of innovative standards in housing technology. Building codes which prescribe construction techniques often become obsolete and prevent the use of the best available method. An alternative approach, to specify the performance desired, leaves the designer free to select the means and also increases the consideration paid to human needs.

Increasingly Human Benefits of Housing Technology.
U.S. Senator Jacob Javits, Remarks on introduction of text of bill (3011), *Congressional Record*, 13 May 71, pp. S6837-39. Proposal for a National Institute on Building Sciences to reorient housing technology.

Constraining Technology: An Historical Study.
Joseph I. Lieberman, *The Scorpion and the Tarantula: The Struggle to Control Atomic Energy, 1945-1949* (3012) (Boston: Houghton-Mifflin, 1970) 460 pp., $8.95. Present-day strategy for social constraints on technology should be grounded in historical insights into the operation of social and institutional drives. This study of the failure of the Acheson-Lilenthal-Baruch Plan analyzes personal factors in the policy process but stops short of disclosing the unexpressed motives and power relationships which may be presumed to influence events. We may hope for a strengthened policy process which will incorporate a deeper understanding of the social character of technology. Lieberman's account is a highly promising step in this direction.

International Institutions and Technology.
Eugene B. Skolnikoff, "Technology and the Future Growth of International Organizations" (3013), *Technology Review*, Vol. 73, No. 8 (Jun 71), pp. 38-47. In-

ternational organizations and the impact of technology, principally in three areas: environmental protection, oceanography, and outer space.

Technology Assessment.
National Academy of Public Administration, "A Technology Assessment System for the Executive Branch" (3014), (Washington: U.S. Government Printing Office, 1970) O-47-213, 48 pp., $.45. Report to the Committee on Science and Astronautics of the U.S. House of Representatives.

Technology Assessment: A Problem and an Approach.
Louis H. Mayo, *The Contextual Approach to Technology Assessment: Implications for "One-Factor Fix" Solutions to Complex Social Problems* (3015) (Apr 71), 90 pp. Program of Policy Studies, George Washington University. Available from National Technical Information System.

International Institute for the Management of Technology.
Being established through the Organization for Economic Cooperation and Development, in Milan, Italy. (3016) Organizing documents and proposals.

National Oceanic Act of 1971.
U.S. Senator Ernest Hollings, Remarks on introduction and text of S. 1986 (3017), *Congressional Record,* 3 June 71, pp. S8068-89. National program of research and development for the oceans, sponsored by Senator Hollings and six others.

Technology Review.
Massachusetts Institute of Technology, (3018) Published monthly, nine issues per year. Subscriptions, $9.00 domestic, $10.00 foreign, from Room E19-430, MIT, cambridge, Mass. 02139. John I. Mattill, Editor.

Military to Civilian Conversion.
Steven R. Rivkin, "The Commonwealth and International Library," *Technology Unbound: Transferring Scientific and Engineering Resources from Defense to Civilian Purposes* (3019) (N.Y.: Pergamon Press, 1968), xiii + 102 pp. A useful summary of the effects of resource reallocation on scientists and engineers.

Technology and Social Purpose.
Glenn T. Seaborg, "The Erewhon Machine; Possibilities for Reconciling Goals by Way of New Technology" (3020), address, 21 April 71, 16 pp.

Technology Assessment.
Hugh Folk, "The Role of Technology Assessment in Public Policy" (3021), Paper for the American Association for the Advancement of Science, 29 Dec 69, 10 pp.

Reinterpretation of Economic Development.
Stephen F. Hochschild, "Technical Assistance and International Development:
A Need for Fundamental Change" (3022). Call for the third world to break the
intellectural and cultural monopoly which holds it in thrall. Paper, 11 pp., Center
for Studies in Education and Development, Harvard University.

The Institutional Legacy of Prometheus.
Alvin M. Weinberg, "Social Institutions and Nuclear Energy" (3023), *Science,*
Vol. 177 (7 July 72), pp. 27-34. Nuclear energy technology poses risks of environmental contamination by radioactive wastes which will commit mankind to eternal
vigilance and stable institutions to maintain deposits of hazardous materials in
perpetuity. Eugene Wigner had compared the commitment to continuous control
of nuclear byproducts to that which men made in embarking on permanent culti-
vation of the land. "Before agriculture, social institutions hardly required the
long-lived stability that we now take so much for granted. . . . In the same sense,
though on a much more sophisticated plane, the knowledge and care that goes into
the proper building and operation of nuclear plants and their subsystems is something that we are committed to forever, so long as we find no other practical energy source of infinite extent." (p. 34)

Redirecting Technology.
Hyman G. Rickover, "Humanistic Technology" (3024), Address, London, 27
Oct 65, 26 pp. Influence of attitudes on use of technology.

Advance Consideration of Social Impact in Planning Research.
Federation of American Societies for Experimental Biology, "A Study of
the Rationale and Techniques for Long-Range Technological Forecasting
in the Biological and Medical Sciences" (3025), 15 Mar 64, 52 pp.

Historical Example of Social Control of Technology.
Noel Perrin, "Giving Up the Gun" (3026), *The New Yorker,* 20 Nov 65, pp. 211-
228. Control of firearms in 17th-century Japan, an early example of social con-
straint of technology.

Decline of Public Confidence in Technology.
U.S. Senator Joseph Montoya, "Science, Research, and Our Heritage of
Progress" (3027), *Congressional Record* (1 Nov 71), S17274-75. Charges
that wasteful military development programs have destroyed public confidence in technology and recommends a Cabinet-level office to achieve
more socially beneficial results from research through stronger management, in order to restore full employment of technical manpower.

Professionalism Narrowly Conceived.
Philip N. Alger, N.A. Christensen, and Sterling P. Olmsted, *Ethical Problems
in Engineering* (3028) (New York: John Wiley and Sons, 1965) xix + 299 pp.

Evidence regarding the state of concern about engineering and society in 1965; conception of ethics as a professional canon, lack of concern about social impact of technology. The above title was sponsored by the Ethics Committee of the American Society for Engineering Education.

Major Compendium on Technology Assessment.
U.S. House of Representatives, Committee on Science and Astronautics, *Technology Assessment* (3029) Hearings before the Subcommittee on Science, Research, and Development, Nov-Dec 69 (91st Congress, 1st Session), 501 pp. An excellent sampling of opinions.

Appraising Impacts of Technology.
National Academy of Sciences, *Technology: Processes of Assessment and Choice* (3030) Committee on Science and Astronautics, U.S. House of Representatives, 91st Congress, 1st Session, Committee Print (U.S.G.P.O., 1969), xiv + 163 pp., $0.75.

Legislative Oversight of Technology.
Congressman John W. Davis, "Technology Assessment and the Congress" (3031), *Congressional Record,* 13 Dec 71, H12396-97. Rationale for the creation of the Office of Technology Assessment embodied in pending legislation.

The Unfathomable Social Dimension of Technology.
Eli Ginzberg, ed., *Technology and Social Change* (3032) (Columbia University Press, 1964) vii + 158 pp., $4.50.

Role of Institutions in Technological Change.
U.S. Department of Commerce, *Technological Innovation: Its Environment and Management* (3033) (Washington: U.S. Government Printing Office, 1972), 83 pp. $1.25. Report submitted in 1967 by a panel headed by Robert A. Charpie, of the Union Carbide Corporation, now of the Cabot Corporation, on institutional factors in technological innovation. According to Daniel Greenberg's *Science and Government Report* (8014) , the Charpie study "was the most frequently cited document in the marathon technology studies that the Nixon Administration set in motion last fall under the direction of William M. Magruder.

The Uncertain Future of Technology.
Eugene S. Schwartz, *Overskill; The Decline of Technology in Modern Civilization* (3034) (Chicago: Quadrangle Books, 1971) xi + 338 pp., bibliog., $8.95. The author, a former senior scientist at the Illinois Institute of Technology, here has issued a broad-front challenge to the belief that more technology can devise remedies for the side-effects of previous technology. He is skeptical about technology assessment and other future-oriented procedures because they tend to extrapolate the past into the

future. The early part of the book cites the role of technology in growth, transportation, energy, pollution control, and war, seeking to show that in each case the application of technology has created more problems than it has solved. Thus technology seems to face a dead end, unless, perhaps, institutional transformations can change its character.

Call for New Profession.
Michael S. Baram, "Social Control of Science and Technology" (3035), *Science,* Vol. 172 (7 May 71), pp. 535-39. Advocates the creation of a new profession to regulate the development of technology in the public interest.

Cultural Interpretation of Engineering Unemployment.
Alvin Rudoff and Dorothy Lucken, "The Engineer and His Work: A Sociological Perspective," (3036), *Science,* Vol. 172 (11 June 71), pp. 1103-8. This sociological analysis explores characteristics of engineers laid off in California between 1963 and 1965, finds resistance to continuing education in that group, and concludes that "the engineer and his work seem to be in deep trouble." Two causes are hinted at: virtually all engineers are employed by organizations, which has precluded the development of ethics akin to those of the self-employed professions, and "the environment in which the engineer works is somewhat akin to an intellectual concentration camp."

Institutional Metamorphosis.
Deborah Shapley, "R&D Conversion: Former NASA Lab Now Working on Transportation" (3037) , *Science,* Vol. 171 (22 Jan 71), pp. 268-69. Describes conversion of the Electronics Research Center of NASA into the Transportation Systems Center of the Department of Transportation.

Redeploying Technical Resources.
U.S. Senate, 92nd Congress, 1st Sess., Committee on Labor and Public Welfare, Hearings: *National Science Foundation Conversion Programs, 1971.* 441 pp. Also S. 32 and remarks in the *Congressional Record* by Senator Kennedy (14 Aug 70; 16 March 71, S3225-231; 10 Nov 71, S18004-5), Congressman Eilberg (8 Sept 71, E9272-73), and Congressman Giaimo (10 Feb 71, H633-644). (3038)

Restating Governmental Interest in Technology.
Richard M. Nixon, "The Importance of Our Investment in Science and Technology—A Message to the Congress" (3039) , *Congressional Record* (16 March 72), H2144-48. While some members of the technical community welcomed a Presidential message on technology that was positive in tone, governmental efforts fall far short of what would be required to mobilize talents the society possesses to address the problems it has

acknowledged. As anthropologist George Pettitt observed in *Prisoners of Culture* (403) (N.Y.: Scribner's, 1970), "The United States has reached a cultural stage where jobs as well as goods are manufactured, and it would make sense to manufacture jobs to fit the people who need them, rather than to go on turning out jobs blindly and screaming at the unemployed, and especially the unemployed young, that they must grow to fit some job that is available, or is believed to be available." (p. 220)

Technology on the Wane.
J. Herbert Hollomon and Alan E. Harger, "America's Technological Dilemma" (3040), *Technology Review,* Vol. 73, no. 9 (July/Aug 71), pp. 30-40. Concentration on military and space technology has undermined subtle institutional processes whereby technology serves social needs and finds expression in industrial innovation. "Perhaps the most important single action that is required is a substantial increase in support for the improvement, both in quality and efficiency, of those public services in which private industry plays only a small role, such as education and the delivery of health care." (pp. 39-40) Also worth quoting in this connection is Barry Commoner's remark in *The Closing Circle; Nature, Man, and Technology* (N.Y.: Alfred A. Knopf, 1971), "It is inconceivable that the United States could find the huge capital resources for the needed reconstruction of industry and agriculture along ecologically sound lines unless we give up our preoccupation with large-scale military activities—which since World War II have preempted most of the nation's disposable income."

Whose Technological Revolution?
Agribusiness Accountability Project, 1000 Wisconsin Avenue, N.W., Washington, D.C. 20007, *Hard Tomatoes Hard Times* (3041) 1972, ix + 308 pp., $2.50. The extensive "land grant college complex" of the United States was the premier experiment in fashioning technology to serve popular needs. Praise for its accomplishments has been a commonplace among leading exponents of science and education policy. Yet, as this report amply documents, the agricultural research enterprise operates with little effective public scrutiny and is far more responsive to corporate interests than to its popular constituencies. The principal bodies cognizant of research policy in this field are the Secretary of Agriculture's Research Policy Advisory Committee (which has no public members) and the Agriculture Division of the National Association of State Universities and Land Grant Colleges, which is made up of all deans of agriculture, 211 heads of state experiment stations, and all deans of extension. The dominance of corporate concerns and the insulation of the entire system from citizen interests are amply documented through an analysis of corporate research support, scholarships, policy influence, and hybrid agencies such as the Nutrition Foundation. The consequence has been an undue preference for mechanization, strikingly exemplified by the

tomatoes of the title, known as MH-1, developed by the University of Florida with "thick walls, firm flesh, and freedom from cracks" for ease in machine harvesting (while green, later "ripened" with ethylene gas). The youthful authors of the report squarely challenge the benign image of agricultural research, while fully conceding the truth of the claims conventionally made on its behalf (p. 34) The displacement of agricultural labor and the decline of rural ways of life have been severe, even if unintended consequences.

"Land grant college research is science for sale. Research is undertaken with a very clear understanding of who will profit, but without the slightest concern for those who will be hurt. It is research that effectively is accountable to none but private interests, and ultimately it is corrupt of purpose." It is a sorry indication of the complacency of our institutions and their limited capacity for self-repair that such a report should originate outside the system and draw to so slight an extent on economics, sociology, and policy analysis. It is open to criticism for giving too simple an account for the factors involved in the great postwar imigra-tion to the cities, but it is likely to focus new attention on the social impact of prevailing agricultural research priorities and the character of the institutions in-volved. Again, the flabbiness of our prestigious and vastly self-satisfied research policy community appears in stark relief, when a six-month commando raid, carried out mostly by students, can make a shambles of some of its most cherished certitudes.

TECHNOLOGICAL AND COMMUNICATIONS INSTITUTIONS

National Environmental Data System.
Senator Philip Hart, Remarks on introduction and text of S.1858 (30000), *Congressional Record*, 13 May 71, pp. S6836-37. All agencies of the Federal Government and their contractors and grantees would be required to make available to a central office all "information, knowledge, and data on the environment," de-fined as "those facts which are significant, accurate, reliable, appropriate, and useful in decision-making in environmental affairs." The scope and potential in-stitutional impact of this proposal are immense, calling for careful consideration in many quarters of the scientific community.

International Application of Communications Technology to Economic Geography.
John Hanessian, Jr., and John M. Logsdon, "Earth Resources Technology Satel-lite; Securing International Participation" (30001) *Astronautics & Aeronautics*, Aug 70, Reprint no. 10 (Sep 70), Program of Policy Studies in Science and Tech-nology, George Washington University, 8 pp.

Unsuccessful Attempt to Establish Academic Job Bank.
George E. Arnstein, "MATCH: Square Pegs for Square Holes" (30002), *Phi Delta Kappan*, (Nov 65), pp. 122-125. Lack of funding and uncoopera-tive attitude of employing institutions killed an early effort by the Associ-

ation of Higher Education to create a national job service. The effort was continued as "Search" under sponsorship of the National Education Association, but that, too, was discontinued in 1970.

Computerized Vacancy Reports.
Ultrasystems, Inc., Report to Office of Policy, Evaluation, and Research, Manpower Administration, U.S. Department of Labor, *An Evaluation of Results and Effectiveness of Job Banks* (30003) ca 250 pp. Describes progress in introducing computerized techniques to operations of the Employment Service, and factors limiting similar development on a statewide basis or for use by other employment agencies.

Program on Technology and Society.
Harvard University, Cambridge, Mass. 02138. Numerous special studies and annual reports. Director, Emmanuel Mesthene. Terminated in 1972. (3.02138)

4. Economic Functions of Society

THE DECLINE AND FALL OF THE AMERICAN EMPIRE

Sabbaticals for Social Betterment.
Xerox Corporation, "Make It Better; Xerox Social Service Leave Program" (4000) pamphlet, 24 pp. The Xerox Corporation has established a program of one-year leaves with full pay to employees seeking to contribute to social betterment. The applicant's supervisor need not approve an application, which is rated by a seven-member committee whose awards are not reviewed by higher authority. Recipients must work with nonprofit nonpartisan organizations, and will not be required to submit progress reports. (Also "The Why of Xerox," *Saturday Review,* 14 Aug 71, pp. 53-54)

Toward Socially Responsible Corporations.
Project on Corporate Responsibility (4001), 1609 Connecticut Avenue, N.W., Washington, D.C. 20009. *News and Thoughts,* issued at intervals. Other documents.

The Reformist Personality.
Articles on Ralph Nader. (4002) . Thoughtful interview on techniques for achieving social responsiveness in corporations, *New York Times,* 24 Jan 71; Julius Duscha, "Stop in the Public Interest!" *New York Times Magazine,* 21 March 71; "Nader's Raiders Put the Washington Press Corps to Shame," *Progressive* (April 71); and Richard Armstrong, "The Passion That Rules Ralph Nader," *Fortune* (May 71), p. 144ff.

Responsiveness of Corporations.
Senator Frank Moss, "Project on Corporate Responsibility" (4003), *Congressional Record* (20 May 71), S7492-96.

Business Appraises Social and Cultural Trends.
General Electric Company, *Our Future Business Environment: Developing Trends and Changing Institutions* (4004) (April 68) 67 pp.; *Our Future Business Environment; A Re-Evaluation* (4005) (July 69) 43 pp.

NEW STATEments.
Reappraising international economic development. Three issues published in its first year by the Canadian University Service Overseas (1971-72). R.H.D. Sallery, Editor-in-chief. From the original statement of purpose: "What role do multinational corporations, military alliances, trade and tariff preferences and even technical and financial 'assistance' play in the creation of development and underdevelopment? This is what NEW STATEments is about—about development in broadest context." Correspondence about future issues should be directed to NEW STATEments, P.O. Box 1028, Pointe Claire, Quebec, Canada. (4006)

Interdependence of Nations.
Wilton S. Dillon, *Gifts and Nations* (4007) (Paris: Mouton, 1970) 170 pp. Avail-

able from the Humanities Press, paper, $5.95. Applies anthropological insights about gift exchange to human involvement in social and economic development.

Monitoring Corporate Responsibility.
The Council on Economic Priorities, "Minding the Corporate Conscience; The 1972 Movement for Corporate Responsibility" *Economic Priorities Report* (4008) , Vol. 3, no. 1 (March/April 72), 35 pp., individual subscriptions, $25.00; corporate and institutional subscriptions (ten copies of each number and one copy of each in-depth study) $350. Summarizes shareholder actions and corporate responses to a range of issues.

Conscience and Capital.
Peter Vanderwicken, "G.M.: The Price of Being 'Responsible'" (4009),, *Fortune* (Jan 72), p. 99ff. Explores possible impacts of socially responsive change on the profitability of General Motors. A Public Policy Committee of the Board, chaired by Pittsburgh banker John A. Mayer, has been meeting regularly with experts and other citizens to reconsider the corporation's social posture, leading in turn to the formation of the scientific advisory committee headed by Charles Townes. Suggests that large productivity increases will be needed to offset added costs of safety and pollution abatement measures.

A Focus for Corporate Responsibility.
Peter Vanderwicken, "Change Invades the Boardroom" (4010) , *Fortune* (May 72), p. 156ff. "Directors realize that the corporate system is on trial," Courtney Brown, former dean of the Columbia University Business School, is quoted as saying in this commentary on directors' responsibilities. Lloyd's of London recently stopped insuring directors against potential liabilities for polluting the environment, for example. Institutional investors are rarely represented on boards. Richard H. Jenrette, President of Donaldson, Lufkin & Jenrette, has suggested the establishment of a nonprofit association that would provide directors to represent institutions.

Federal Charters Unlikely to Direct Corporations toward Social Ends.
Henry C. Wallich, "What Future for Corporations?" (4011) , *Congressional Record* (13 Oct 71), E10737-39. Argues that corporations should seek social objectives in order to avert stifling regulation, and regard the cost of so doing not as a toll on their shareholders but as a means of creating desirable externalities for recapture elsewhere in the economy.

Corporate Commitment to Studying Social Needs.
A. W. Clausen, "Bank of America Moves to Set Quality Standard to Gauge Social Ills" (4012) *Congressional Record,* 5 April 71.

A Corporate Social Audit.
David Rockefeller, "The Role of Business in an Era of Growing Accountability" (4013), *Congressional Record,* 24 Jan 72, S314-15. Rockefeller
styles the movement for corporate responsibility a demand "for revision
of the social contract," to which he believes corporations might adapt by
submitting to periodic social audits, increasing use of performance contracting to address social problems, and participating in the development
of new towns.

Economic Misdirection.
Ralph Nader, "A Citizen's Guide to the American Economy" (4014) ,
The New York Review of Books (2 Sept 71), pp. 14-18. Describes six
"sub-markets" through which resources are diverted to uses that have
little human benefit. Correction of abusive procurement practices, monopoly profits, worthless products, and other irregularities in the market
for goods and services could generate vast savings to be applied to more
urgent social needs.

An Inventory Crisis in Careers.
Peter F. Drucker, "The New Markets and the New Capitalism" (4015),
The Public Interest, No. 21 (Fall 70), pp. 44-79.

Employment Outlook Summary.
U.S. Department of Labor, "Occupational Outlook Handbook in Brief,
1970-71" (4016) , *Congressional Record* (16 Dec 71), E13667-673.

A New Institution for Assessment of Competitiveness.
Lewis Beman, "How to Tell Where the U.S. Is Competitive" (4017), *Fortune,*
July 72, p. 54ff. Describes various theories of economic advantage in international
trade, especially regarding the role of high technology products, as the occasion
for creating, in the U.S. Department of Commerce, an office to monitor the competitiveness of American business in relation to the introduction of new
technology.

Institutions and Changing Views of Development.
Everett Reimer, "An Institutional Approach to Economic Development" (4018)
CIDOC 69/161 (1969) 6 pp. Institutions which aided development among economically advanced nations thwart the process in the third world today. Reimer
urges the development of conceptual tools to understand the historical process
by which major institutions were introduced, the sociological means by which
they become acceptable, and the limitations which they now place on the search
for alternatives.

CORPORATIONS AND ECONOMIC INSTITUTIONS

Fostering "Consumerism."
President's Committee on Consumer Interests, "Forming Consumer Organizations" (40000) 38 pp. Available from the Office of Consumer Affairs, Washington, D.C. 20506 Includes roster of consumers' associations and consumer offices in state and local government.

An Institutional Antagonist.
John Brooks, "The Marts of Trade: Anti-Corporation" (40001), *The New Yorker* (9 Oct 71), pp. 138-143. Describes the proposal of Thomas B. Mechling and Clement L. Despard for an "anti-corporation" that would seek to earn profits by recovering damages and penalties through legal action against other corporations and governmental bodies. Ralph Nader and others are gradually perfecting techniques of legal action that might be used to compel many different kinds of institutions to perform in the public interest or be subject to penalties.

Call for Institutional Reevaluation.
William L. Casey, Jr., "The Federal Reserve System: A Case Study in Institutional Unresponsiveness" (40002), *Congressional Record,* 28 Sept 71, H8782-83.

Improving the Financial Structure.
Committee on Financial Institutions, *Report of the Committee on Financial Institutions to the President of the United States* (40003) (U.S.G.P.O., 1963) viii + 66 pp., $0.25. The sophistication with which economists develop and criticize policy toward financial institutions contrasts painfully with the conventional approach toward knowledge institutions.

Capital Investment and Social Improvement.
Harvey Shapiro, "Wall Street's New 'Social Responsibility' Funds" (40004), *Saturday Review,* 26 Aug 72, pp. 43-45. Describes Pax World Fund, Third Century Fund, First Spectrum Fund, and Social Dimensions Fund—mutual funds seeking to reorient investment toward socially responsive companies. According to Professor Roger Murray of the Columbia University Graduate School of Business, "the funds represent a new and very material form of pressure on managements. Corporations will feel on the defensive with other stockholders if the social funds don't approve their stock." (p. 44) In a related development, with potentially greater impact, President Lawrence S. Phillips, of Phillips-Van Heusen (1971 sales: $255 million), has appointed eight young middle managers to recommend how the company should vote the proxies of the ninety-odd corporations included in its $11-million pension-fund portfolio. According to *Fortune,* Sept 72, "If other companies follow suit, Phillips says, within a decade there'll be more 'good guys' than bad ones on the corporate scene." (p. 36)

5. Human Service, Community Development

"VIVA LA CAUSA"

National Service.
U.S. Senator Fred Harris, Remarks on introduction and text of S. 1064 (5000), *Congressional Record,* 2 Mar 71, pp. S2247-251. Foundation on Youth Participation proposed as an executive branch agency by nine Democratic Senators, to make grants to public and private agencies which sponsor programs for youth that involve their active participation in planning and implementation.

Social Action.
Timothy J. Cooney and James Haughton, *It's Up to YOU; A Guide to Changing the System* (5001) (N.Y.: Ives Washburn, Inc., 1971), xiii + 104 pp., $4.25. The founders of "Fight Back," a Harlem campaign on behalf of equal opportunity in the construction unions, describe practical steps whereby citizens may exert pressure for change in political and economic institutions.

Institutionalization of Sex Roles.
Barbara A. Brown, Thomas I. Emerson, Gail Falk, and Ann E. Freedman, "The Equal Rights Amendment: A Constitutional Basis for Equal Rights for Women" (5002), *Congressional Record,* 5 Oct 71, S15840-869. Reprinted from the *Yale Law Journal.*

Youth Service.
The Cincinnati Experience (5003), Reprint from the *Cincinnati Alumnus,* article from the *Cincinnati Enquirer* 10 May 71, 8 pp. Also "Drug Program Booklet," May 71, 10 pp., and "A Proposal for the Reclamation of Solid Waste," 14 pp. A bridge from the university to middle America; student dialogue with citizens on issues of social concern.

Student Intern Experience.
Rayburn M. Hanzlik, "The University of Virginia and Community Development; an Institutional Survey" (5004) (Aug 69) 55 pp. Survey for the Center for the Study of Science, Technology, and Public Policy, University of Virginia. Student intern evaluates opportunities for partnership between his university and its community. A project under the Resource Development Internship Program of the Southern Regional Education Board, supported by the Economic Development Administration, Tennessee Valley Authority, and Office of Economic Opportunity.

National Political Internship Program.
Senator Hubert Humphrey, Remarks on introduction and text of S.1410 (5005), *Congressional Record,* 30 Mar 71, pp. S4071-72. National internship program to offer students practical political involvement with elected officials on local, state, and federal levels.

National Service.
Congressman Jonathan Bingham, National service amendment to Selective

Service Act (5006), *Congressional Record,* 30 Mar 71, 6 pp., and 1 Apr 71, 3 pp. Discussion includes a memorandum on constitutional issues. The amendment was defeated on a voice vote, 1 April 1971.

Student Assignment Opportunities in a Rural Action Organization.
National Farmers Organization "You Don't Have to Leave the Country to Do a World of Good" (5007), 10 pp., Field Staff, National Farmers' Organization, Corning, Iowa 50841.

National Service.
Donald J. Eberly, ed., *National Service; Report of a Conference* (5008) (New York: Russell Sage Foundation, 1968) ix + 598 pp.

Youth Council Proposed for Executive Office of the President.
Congressmen William Steiger, Remarks on introduction and text of bill (5009), *Congressional Record,* 7 Apr 71, pp. H2623-24. Congressman Steiger's bill would provide a five-member senior policy and program review council. Also, statement by Senator William Brock on S.1539, companion legislation in the Senate, *Congressional Record,* 14 Apr 71, pp. S4757-68.

Reorganization of Governmental Volunteer Programs.
U.S. Senator Harrison Williams, Comments on Presidential Reorganization Plan No. 1 (5010), *Congressional Record,* 29 Apr 71, pp. S5766-770. Also a further statement in opposition to the plan, *Congressional Record,* 21 May 71, p. S57572. The plan went into effect 1 July 71 with the creation of ACTION, the new volunteer agency.

Proposed National Youth Service Act.
U.S. Senator Mark Hatfield, Remarks on introduction and text of S.1777 (5011), *Congressional Record,* 5 May 71, pp. S6247-49.

National Service.
Donald J. Eberly, "The Estimated Effect of a National Service Program on Public Service Manpower Needs, Youth Employment, College Attendance, and Marriage Rates," and "National Service Research Topics" (5012). Paper for the Russell Sage Foundation (Jan 70) 52 pp.

National Service.
Fred Best, "A National Public Service Program" (5013), Mar 71, 16 pp. From preliminary recommendations to the White House Conference on Youth, Task Force on Economy and Employment.

National Service.
National Service Secretariat, *Newsletter* (5014) Published quarterly. Annual rate (tax-deductible contribution) $5.00. Reviews of pertinent literature and government and other proposals on all aspects of service-learning. Donald J. Eberly is editor.

Directories of Black Community Activities and Centers.
Afram Associates, Inc., 68-72 East 131st Street, New York, New York 10037, *Action Library* (5015). A great variety of publications is available, annual subscription $50.00. President, Preston Wilcox.

State Internship Office.
North Carolina State Board of Higher Education, North Carolina Internship Office (5016) Robert L. Sigmon, Director, 116 West Jones St., Raleigh, North Carolina 27603. Publications available include "Student Internship Programs in North Carolina, Summer 1970," 46 pp.; Lawrence Whitfield, "Internship Program Profiles in North Carolina Summer 1970," 46 pp.; and Robert L. Sigmon, "Service-Learning, An Educational Style" (July 70), 14 pp.

Child Development Services.
Congressman John Brademas, "The Comprehensive Child Development Program" (5017), *Congressional Record*, 30 Nov 71, H11517-11524. Also S19899-900.

Urban Problems—The Ethnic Dimension.
National Center for Urban Ethnic Affairs, 702 Lawrence Street, N.E., Washington, D.C. 20017. *Working Class and Ethnic Priorities* (5018) 25 pp. Also *All Men Are Brothers*, "Report on Urban Ethnic Affairs," Task Force on Urban Problems, U.S. Catholic Conference, 10 Nov 70, 117 pp. Also "Evolving Patterns of Ethnicity in American Life," 1 June 71, 60 pp. and occasional newsletter (5. 20017).

Proposal: International Cities Institute.
Harry Blaney, Office of the Chairman, Council on Environmental Quality, The White House, Washington, D.C. (5019) 7 pp., 1971. Proposes an operating agency with systems analysis capability, to respond to requests from city governments for studies of the interrelations of functions in urban areas.

Community Involvement and the Urban University.
Kermit C. Parsons and Georgia K. Davis, "The Urban University and its Urban Environment" (5020) , *Minerva*, Vol. 9 (1971), pp. 361-385. General survey of community services undertaken by urban universities in the United States.

The Threadbare Fabric of Community.
National Commission on the Causes and Prevention of Violence, Final Report, *To Establish Justice, to Insure Domestic Tranquility* (5021) (U.S.G.P.O., 1969 0-371-832) xxxii + 338 pp., $1.50.

The Futility of Anarchism: The Political Dropout Syndrome.
Benjamin R. Barber, *Superman and Common Men; Freedom, Anarchy, and the Revolution* (5022) (N.Y.: Praeger, 1971), 125 pp., $5.00. Those

who seek to enlarge the possibilities of actual change must forego the poetry of pure ideals, if they are to avoid the sterile trap of anarchistic political attitudes. Anarchist movements have rarely included men of practical ability and have repeatedly failed to gain a popular following because they have unrealistically exhorted men to be better than they actually are. "No revolutionaries can compromise with their enemies and survive, but the anarchists are unwilling to compromise with their followers. They expect men to endure a physical hunger to quench a spiritual thirst." (p. 22) Unable to win the common man to his program, the anarchist confides it to criminals or resorts to theatrical violence. Barber, a member of the political science faculty at Rutgers, offers this critique of anarchism in an effort to establish that social institutions will not be reformed by desperado raids, but only by reconstituting democracy across a broad front. What frustrates so many present-day social aspirations is the indifference of the majority, which is nonetheless acknowledged as the ultimate source of political legitimacy. Seemingly the majority violates no constitutional precepts because it restrains no-one's freedom. Whoever defines freedom as the absence of physical contraints on movement is bound by the logic of our legal order to respect the majority, and if he finds it immoveable, to be driven into opposition. Barber's considerations of the political aspirations of the oppositional youth culture leads him to a strikingly fundamental critique of conventional liberal concepts of freedom, upon which majoritarian tyranny is based.

"All his life man is imprisoned by his institutions," wrote Rousseau. Freedom is nothing if not a choice among desirable possibilities, which our institutions do not offer. The freedom to attend college, for example, is spurious if it entails complete acceptance of middle-class social allegiances, for then the only alternative is dropping out altogether. Genuine freedom requires tension among alternative possibilities, and conflict as to which potentiality will be realized. A majority that is sustained by the manipulation of opinion violates this "intentionalist" principle of freedom even if no physical constraints are imposed. A society that denies men an affirmative sense of working out their own destinies cannot be considered democratic in these terms. A somnolent majority manipulated by elites excludes the change forces of society, which then contend fruitlessly for its favor. Barber identifies three forces seeking social change: the economically disadvantaged, those seeking racial justice, and those seeking to enhance humane values. If these strands are not somehow woven together, one likely result would be anarchy, of which there are abundant portents in central cities. Another would be fascism. The effect of uniting these forces, precarious and difficult, would be to recreate democracy, through a wide reawakening of consciousness—"the securing of conditions that permit common men to make autonomous decisions about their collective welfare." (p. 121)

In this way Barber traces failures of allegiance, which the young display by dropping out or rebelling, to the emptiness at the center of our democracy. An era of regeneration could regain their loyalty and draw the revolutionary forces into creative, sustaining discourse with society as a whole. But our present institutions seem dead set against such a result. For example, by confining career choice in sterile patterns, we guarantee that the graduates of tomorrow will simply extend and maintain the institutional system of the present. Thus the guidance counselor, with his recipe book of occupations, backed up by expert hiring forecasts, directs the stream of talent into rigid molds. The assumptions of manpower planners, and prescriptive problem-solving generally, are beautifully revealed in Barber's penetrating analysis of the conventions of forecasting. "The mechanist, by depicting the future as a kind of road map on which the free man charts routes appropriate to his needs and wants, projects his determinist assumptions about the past onto the future. Time is laid out like a fourth physical dimension; man's present is but a line moving across time, changing future into past as it moves. The future is a given, there, existent, but not yet here; or, rather, we are not yet there. Freedom, in this closed framework, is mere choice, and choice is simply selection among givens. But for the intentionalist, the future—quite literally—is not. It must be created. Man's freedom lies in his capacity to create it: what will be is what we will." (p. 59)

New Directions in Legal Education.
Association of American Law Schools, One Dupont Circle, N.W., Washington, D.C. 20036. *Training for the Public Professions of the Law* (5023) Proceedings of the 1971 Annual Meeting, Part I, Section II, 249 pp.

Professional Education: An Institutional Appraisal.
Lewis B. Mayhew, *Changing Practices in Education for the Professions* (5024), Research Monograph No. 17, Southern Regional Education Board, 130 Sixth Street, N.W., Atlanta, Georgia 30311. vii + 82 pp., $2.25. Discusses directions of change in the professions, questions of curriculum design and relations with other programs in the university, and the response of institutions.

Reform Program for Professional Education.
Allen B. Rosenstein, Education Development Program, School of Engineering, University of California at Los Angeles, *A Study of a Profession and Professional Education* (5025) Dec 68, 174 pp. Advocates the development of a unified professional curriculum based upon design, applied humanities, and applied mathematics.

HUMAN SERVICE INSTITUTIONS AND PROFESSIONS

Institutional Outlets for Professional Responsibility.
Samuel C. Palmer, III, "Free from Politics: A National Legal Services

Corporation: The Legal Profession's Responsibility" (50000), *Congressional Record*, 23 Sept 71, E9957-960.

Federal Regulation of Private Foundations.

Committee on Banking and Currency, U.S. House of Representatives, 92nd Congress, 1st Session, "The Fifteen Largest United States Foundations: Financial Structure and the Impact of the Tax Reform Act of 1969" (50001), Committee Print, 15 July 71, 27 pp. "U.S. foundations are once again at the crossroads. For almost eight years after a House subcommittee, under my chairmanship, began documenting improper activities, their reaction was to ignore the Congress and resist reform. The result was a reform imposed on foundations by Congress. If the facts developed in this report continue to hold true for succeeding years, it will be abundantly clear that foundations have been led only part way into the twentieth century." These comments by Wright Patman indicate his faith in the federal tax code as an instrument of institutional "reform." Instead socially responsive change has become less likely because foundation officers fear further Congressional action and the foundations are snared in a web of contradictory legal technicalities.

Obsolescence of Penal Institutions.

Louis E. Wolfson, "Prisons: Colleges for Crime" (50002), *Congressional Record*, 14 Oct 71, H9616-18.

Unconstitutionality of Practices of Correctional Institutions.

U.S District Judge Robert H. Merhige, Jr., Opinion in *Robert J. Landman et al. vs. M. L. Royster*, entered into the *Congressional Record* for 12 Nov 71 by Congresswoman Abzug of New York, E12134-148. (50003)

Legal Services Corporation.

U.S. Senator James Pearson, "To Protect the Rights of the Poor: The Legal Services Corporation Act of 1971" (50004), *Congressional Record*, 12 Oct 71, S16186-89.

Institutional Failure in Rural Development.

National Academy of Sciences, "A National Rural Center: Applying Science and Technology to Improve the Quality of Rural Life" (50005), *Congressional Record*, 30 Sept 71, S15510-18.

Institutional Reform—The Prison System.

Jack Waugh, "Prisons: Changing a System That Does Not Work" (50006), *Congressional Record*, 18 Jan 72, E107-115. A series of excellent articles from *The Christian Science Monitor*.

Fostering Social Responsiveness in the Professions.

Allen B. Rosenstein, "National Professions Foundation" (50007), *Congressional Record*, 15 Dec 71, S21682-84, with accompanying remarks by U.S. Senator Hubert H. Humphrey. "A National Professions Foundation should be established to provide direction for the discharge of the social responsibilities of the professions and to function in parallel with the National Science Foundation and the new National Foundation on the Arts and the Humanities."

Manpower—Where Institutions Fail.
Leonard P. Adams, "Cornell Studies in Industrial and Labor Relations, Vol. 16" *The Public Employment Service in Transition, 1933-1968; Evolution of a Placement Service into a Manpower Agency* (50008) (New York State School of Industrial and Labor Relations, 1969) xv +246 pp., $6.50 cloth, $3.50 paper. The Federal-State Employment Service, with 2,350 local offices and an annual appropriation of $500 million, operated through the 1950's almost entirely as a placement service. In the 1960's its mandate was broadened to include remedial training aimed especially at members of disadvantaged groups. This study offers an anatomy of this change and of resistance to it within the decentralized system of agencies.

The discrepancy between the official view of public employment services and the way they in fact perform is apparently of long standing. One of the main reasons for establishing public labor exchanges was to secure public acceptance for unemployment insurance, the beneficiaries of which needed a place where they could register and certify that they were seeking jobs. Funds for the operation of the exchanges were originally derived mainly from payroll taxes for unemployment insurance. (p. 21) These services were greatly expanded during World War II but could not assemble adequate staff and were ignored by many employers. (p. 29) A network for professional and technical positions was gradually developed during the 1950's, which led the Employment Service to inaugurate placement services at professional meetings. Although still used by a number of learned and scientific societies, changes in location of the annual meetings rule out any continuity in such services. (p. 41) In 1961, under President Kennedy's direction, local offices took on additional responsibilities in order to function as "community manpower centers," but the inadequacies of job information severely limited their effectiveness. (p. 56) Private employment agencies have consistently opposed both administrative and legislative moves to strengthen the public Employment Service. (p. 63)

The Employment Service accounted for about 16 percent of the placements in industry in 1962-63, direct application for 36 percent, relatives and friends for 23 percent, newspaper ads 11 percent, fee-charging agencies 4 percent, and all others 10 percent. (p. 77) Each year approximately 250,000 of the 6 or 7 million placements arranged by these services are in the professional-technical category, and half of these are short-term placements of teachers and nurses.

Professor Adams is skeptical about the computerized job information bank recommended by the Commission on Technology, Automation, and Economic Progress in 1966. The "half-life" of information on specific jobseekers or openings is about five weeks, which is about as long as it would take to analyze and clear entries for a national system. Also, voluntary computer systems rarely exceed 50-70 percent coverage. Resort to computers would not eliminate the need for brokers to resolve differences between jobseekers and employers. "The proposed system would probably work best for professional, technical, and highly skilled job candidates and permanent openings in those categories that have remained unfilled for some time. . . . All things considered, it is likely that computers can best be used in selected occupational fields and for experienced workers who have skills in demand." (pp. 172-173).

While the public Employment Service has not altogether succeeded in reorienting its staff efforts to the hard-core unemployed, service to the disadvantaged has become enough of a dominant concern to provoke doubt as to its capability to serve the highly skilled. Quite apart from wondering how priorities could be maintained in the orientation of a decentralized service operating under loose federal control, one might ask whether private, fee-charging agencies could be led to coordinate their efforts with such a system, or how it could be extended to the not-for-profit services of professional societies and various university associations or consortia. Notwithstanding the response to social needs on the part of the Employment Service, it is beset by inconsistencies if not conflicts of purpose, confusions in organization and budgeting, and inadequacies of information that cripple its performance as an agency.

Manpower Institutions Resisting Social Change.

Stanley H. Ruttenberg and Jocelyn Gutchess, "Policy Studies in Employment and Welfare, No. 5" *The Federal-State Employment Service; A Critique* (50009) (Johns Hopkins University Press, 1970) x + 104 pp., paper $1.95. The senior author, who served as Assistant Secretary of Labor in the Johnson Administration. describes a group of "institutional barriers" which he thinks prevent the Employment Service from achieving its potential as the primary instrument of national manpower policy. These include the basic method of funding (by a tax on employers), the legislative mandate to serve all jobseekers (which prevents the Service from observing priorities), its organizational status as a coordinate of the unemployment insurance service, burdensome procedures, reliance on state civil service systems and staff training schemes, and the powerful but obstructive Interstate Conference of Employment Security Agencies. He styles the Employment Service "the manpower institution which has been a formidable roadblock to social change." While he is able to cite some new programs which he regards as having been successful, it is clear that the Employment Service is beset with organizational problems which no constituency is presently pressing to eliminate.

Mr. Ruttenberg cites with approval a budget order of October, 1968 reducing services to professional and high-level jobseekers. He argues that the Service must concentrate on disadvantaged and hard-core unemployed, lacking resources to serve all comers. He concludes with a series of recommendations for organizational adjustments (pp. 87-103).

Governmental Chaos and Manpower Programs.

Stanley Ruttenberg assisted by Jocelyn Gutchess, "Policy Studies in Employment and Welfare Number Two," *Manpower Challenge of the 1970s: Institutions and Social Change* (50010) (Johns Hopkins University Press, 1970) viii + 126 pp., paper, $1.95. The initial focus for the development of new federal manpower programs in the 1960's was retraining for skilled workers threatened by technological obsolescence, in response to the belief that automation threatened their jobs. Skilled workers seemed able to change specialties and avoided substantial unemployment. The Federal Government recognized that needs for assistance were instead much greater among the unskilled and the unemployed poor. This led to a succession of legislative enactments and a bewildering array of federal programs which became steadily harder to plan and coordinate. The author, who served as director of the Manpower Administration of the U.S. Department of Labor from 1965 through 1968, describes with some pride a creature called the "Cooperative Area Manpower Planning System" which sought to coordinate manpower plans of seven federal agencies through a three-level tier of some 400 committees, some with as many as 100 members. It was merely voluntary even for federal agencies (only a few bureaus of HEW and Interior participated, for example), included in its terms of reference about one-third of the federal manpower programs and no private ones, was infected with an air of unreality from the start, and never obtained significant representation from state and local governments. (pp. 48-51) The machinery was solemnly set in motion and operated for several years although it did not include the OEO Comprehensive Work and Training Program or the Model Cities Program. It seems to have been little more than an elaborate theater for jurisdictional rivalries among the Employment Service, other units of the Labor Department, and other federal agencies. A sweeping reorganization of manpower agencies had been proposed in 1964, but when Ruttenberg took office he was forced to disclaim it by Congressional overseers friendly to pre-existing baronies. After manful efforts to make the existing non-system work he planned to convert the three-tier system to a four-tier system by introducing eight regional manpower coordinators. Eager plans were made to have the reorganization (which had many other features, some quite reasonable) announced by the President, but this merely gave the plan's opponents a conspicuous target. The weeks slipped by until the month before the election of 1968 and the President took no action. This prompted Secretary of Labor Willard Wirtz to announce it himself, only to be countermanded by the President, precipitating a letter of resignation, which President Johnson refused to accept unless Writz withdrew his reorganization, which he refused to do. (pp. 74-97)

Ruttenberg claims that manpower programs can have quick economic and social impact. "This is one reason why manpower is so important as a tool of economic policy." (p. 21) What he has shown in this saddening recital of the organizational disarray of government is only its impotence, resulting from the intractability of the institutional system.

Civil Service: The Illusion of Control.
Richard K. Irish, "Survival Guide for Washington Bureaucrats" (50011), *Washington Post, Potomac* (16 April 72), p. 11ff. The "hidden job market" of the Federal Government operates "through a grapevine of intelligence, an old boy network, or in the specialized channels of your craft, skill, or field," according to the Vice President of TransCentury Corp., who operates a counseling and placement service for "judgment jobs". The vast, costly personnel establishment, beloved of civics textbooks and despised by all operating executives, is hardly ever called upon except to give grudging approval after employment decisions are taken.

The Bankruptcy of the Federal Unemployment Effort.
Lawyers' Committee for Civil Rights under Law, *Falling Down on the Job: The United States Employment Service and the Disadvantaged* (50012) (June 71), 129 pp. of unrelieved criticism.

An Innovation in Job Information and Placement.
INTERCEPT and SOCIOCOM were founded over two years ago to provide accurate and current employment information in education and social-economic development. These two firms publish information for both the prospective employee and the employer. Their method of operation is simple: they send listings of available positions to job-seekers and send descriptions of candidates to institutions with position openings. INTERCEPT and SOCIOCOM publish all job openings which come to their attention and publish all resumes of candidates who want their descriptions publicly distributed. They are "open systems" with no hidden listings. A candidate may subscribe to INTERCEPT or SOCIOCOM but there is no fee for actual placement.

INTERCEPT publishes listings in higher education and secondary education. Its publications come out in Winter and Spring of each year with information on available teaching positions starting the following September. INTERCEPT's coverage is nationwide and it lists teaching openings in practically all academic and professional fields. INTERCEPT has had over 3,000 individual subscribers since it began. It has published about 1,000 openings since it started. It has just completed in its third publishing season. INTERCEPT also has a number of institutional subscribers, which include libraries, placement offices and academic departments. The individual subscription rate for INTERCEPT is $10.00.

SOCIOCOM publishes monthly listings in social-economic development. Approximately 700 organizations have indicated that they will list openings in SOCIOCOM if jobs become open. These organizations include Model Cities Programs, Community Action Agencies, Community Mental Health programs, Legal Service Programs, Settlement Houses, Consulting Firms and a variety of other organizations. SOCIOCOM covers the whole range of work in the social sector: Administration and Planning, Direct Services, Ecology-Environment, Education, Health and Mental Health, Housing, International Opportunities, Legal Services, Manpower, and Research, Information Systems and Data Processing. Approximately 2,000 individuals have subscribed to SOCIOCOM, and SOCIOCOM has listed approximately 1,000 positions. The individual subscription rates for SOCIOCOM are: 2 months—$10.00, 4 months—$16.00, 6 months—$20.00, 12 months—$25.00.   (5.02138)
Mel Horwitch, President
INTERCEPT/SOCIOCOM
PO Box 317, Harvard Square
Cambridge, MA 02138
Tel: 617-868-4150

Catalyst.
6 East 82nd Street, New York, N. Y. 10028. A national nonprofit organization seeking to improve society's use of educated women, who are barred by conventional employment patterns from combining family and career responsibilities. "Though social and economic problems cry out for the brainpower, dedication, and creativity these women have to offer, much of the investment in their education is going to waste." (5.10028)

Profile of Public Interest Law Firm.
Center for Law and Social Policy. (5.20036), "Legal Matters Pending" and program statement. This firm addresses itself particularly to problems of technology assessment and environmental quality. 1600 20th Street, N.W., Washington, D.C. 20036.

Vocations for Social Change.
Box 13, Canyon, California 94516. Newsletter on opportunities to pursue vocations outside the system of established institutions. Lists job openings and proposals in alternative institutions, education, professions, organizing, media, peace efforts, and apprenticeships. *Workforce Magazine,* annual rate, $10.00. (5.94516)

National Registry for Engineers.
800 Capitol Mall, Sacramento, Calif. 95814. A computerized register of unemployed engineers, operated for the Manpower Administration by the Human Relations Agency of the State of California.   (5.95814)

6. Human and Environmental Well Being

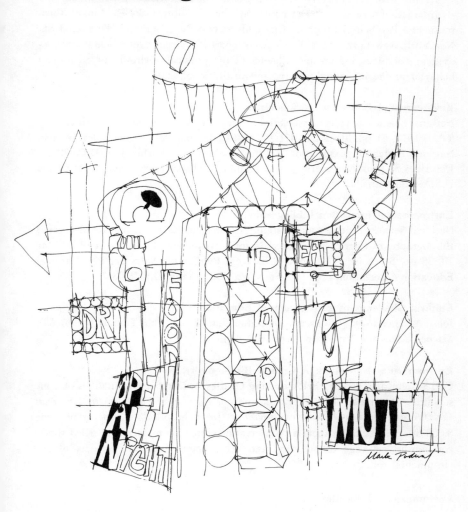

KEEP AMERICA BEAUTIFUL

Environment and Behavior.
(6000) Published quarterly. Subscriptions, $10.00 per year to institutions, $7.00 to individuals; add $1.00 outside North America. Sage Publications, Inc., 275 South Beverly Drive, Beverly Hills, Calif. 90212. "An Interdisciplinary Journal Concerned with the Study, Design, and Control of the Physical Environment and Its Interaction with Human Behavioral Systems." Editor, Gary H. Winkel. Environmental Psychology Program, City University of New York, 33 West 42nd St., New York, New York 10036. The journal reports "rigorous experimental and theoretical work focusing on the influence of the physical environment on human behavior at the individual, group, and institutional scale."

Environmental Education in Schools.
National Science Teachers Association, "Programs in Environmental Education" (6001) 1970, 51 pp. Stock No. 471-14394, $1.50, from Publication Sales Section, National Education Association, 1201 16th St. N.W., Washington, D.C. 20036. Describes 55 projects underway in elementary and secondary schools around the U.S.A. and Canada.

Environmental Education Bibliography.
National Science Teachers Association, "Environmental Education for Everyone; Bibliography of Curriculum Materials for Environmental Studies" (6002), Mar 70, 38 pp. Stock No. 471-14600, $.75, from Publication Sales Section, National Education Association, 1201 16th St. N.W., Washington, D.C. 20036.

Cultural Challenge of Environmental Education.
John A. Gustafson, "Conservation Education Today and Tomorrow" (6003), *Science Education,* Vol. 53, no. 3 (April 69), pp. 187-190.

Environmental Education: A Critical Bibliography.
Carl S. Johnson, David L. Erickson, and Charles A. Dambach, "Qualities of Conservation Materials" (6004), *Transactions of the Thirty-First North American Wildlife and Natural Resources onference,* 14-16 March 1966. Survey of some 8,000 titles of free or inexpensive conservation education materials revealed shortcomings in coverage of pollution and other socially relevant aspects of environmental quality.

Environmental Education.
Massachusetts Audubon Society, "Environmental Education Bibliography" (6005) (1970), 48 pp. Prepared for the U.S. Office of Education. In three sections: preschool to grade 3, grades 4-6, and grades 7-9.

Environmental Education: The Federal Program.
U.S. Office of Education, "Environment Education: Education That Cannot Wait" (6006). (Aug 70), 28 pp. Discussion of policy aims and procedures for implementing the Environmental Education Act of 1970.

Appraising Environmental Problems for Public Understanding.
Committee for Environmental Information, *Environment,* (6007) Issued ten times yearly. Subscriptions, $10.00 in U.S.A.; $12.00 foreign; $7.50 students; P.O. Box 755, Bridgeton, Missouri 63044. Published by the Committee for Environmental Information, 438 N. Skinker Blvd., St. Louis, Mo. 63130. Previously titled *Scientist and Citizen;* editor, Sheldon Novick. The policy of the magazine is to disseminate objective scientific information relevant to political and social issues without bias or prejudgment.

New Journal in Conservation Communications.
Dember Education Research Services, *Environmental Education* (6008) Issued four times yearly. Subscriptions, $7.50 per year; students, $5.00. P.O. Box 1605, Madison, Wisconsin 53701. Editor Clay Shoenfeld is Chairman of the Center for Environmental Communications and Education Studies, University of Wisconsin at Madison.

General Audience Ecology Journal.
Ecology Today (6009) Published monthly. Subscriptions, $5.00 per year, $6.00 overseas, from Ecological Dimensions, Inc., Box 180, West Mystic, Conn. 06388. James A. Hayeland, Editor.

National System of Environmental Research.
Albert H. Teich, "Progress Report on Guidelines for a National Program of Environmental Research Laboratories" (6010), 26 Feb 71, study conducted by the Policy Institute, Syracuse University Research Corporation. Procedures governing a census of environmental research centers operated by the Federal Government. Proposal to create a continuing inventory of environmental research centers in all sectors.

Regional Ecological Knowledge and Advisory Centers.
William R. Ewald, Jr., 1150 Connecticut Avenue, N.W., Washington, D.C. 20036, "Managing the Environment Now for the World Ahead" (6011), 49 pp., 18 Jan 72. The author, a planner and development consultant, believes that universities must invariably fail to provide interdisciplinary contexts to which faculty members would subordinate their professional independence and claims for recognition. Funding for such centers would be very difficult to secure and their findings might be disregarded by major social institutions. He therefore proposes that regional electric utilities provide funding for long-range resource policy planning as an overhead on energy costs, to be supplemented by government and other research support. The paper proposes a "social invention": regional ecological knowledge and advisory centers, operating independently of government and industry. He concludes with a description of Santa Barbara as a model setting for such a center. His proposal that resource research be made part of the rate base of utilities deserves wide consideration.

The Environmental Policy Literature Explosion.
George H. Siehl, "Literature Subsequent to the Environmental Nova" (6012), *Congressional Record,* 27 Sept 71, H8738-743. Review of recent environmental policy literature by a member of the staff of the Environmental Policy Division of the Congressional Research Service, reprinted from *The Library Journal.*

Employment Outlook in Environmental Management.
Odom Fanning, "Vocational Guidance Materials," *Opportunities in Environmental Careers* (6013) (N.Y.: Universal Publishing and Distributing Corporation, 1971), 271 pp. Series of appraisals of career opportunity in environmental sciences, resources and recreation, environmental design, environmental protection, and environmental policy. Draws upon employment forecasts where available but does not attempt an analytic treatment of prospects for job creation. Herbert Bienstock, regional director of the Bureau of Labor Statistics in New York City, has estimated that environment-related activities now employ 656,000 and that this will increase to 1.2 million by 1980 (*New York Times,* 23 May 71), but many others have cautioned that few new jobs have resulted from environmental protection efforts to date.

INSTITUTIONS FOR HEALTH AND ENVIRONMENTAL PROTECTION

Proposal: National System of Environmental Research.
Raymond Bowers, *et al,* "A Program to Coordinate Environmental Research: What Kind of Organization Can Improve the Level of Research on the Environment?" (60000), *American Scientist,* Vol. 59 (Mar-Apr 71) pp. 183-87. Research coordination as a foundation for environmental policy, proposal for a national institute of environmental policy analysis to work in support of the Environmental Protection Agency, also a technical laboratory as a subordinate element of the institute.

Presidential Proposal for Environmental Institute.
President Richard M. Nixon, "First Annual Report on the State of the Nation's Environment" (60001), 8 pp. U.S. House of Representatives (92nd Congress, 2d Session) Doc. No. 92-46. The President's proposals were made pursuant to recommendations of the Environmental Studies Board of the National Academy, but the proposed institute was stillborn.

The Institutional Aspect of Environmental Protection.
Environmental Study Group, Environmental Studies Board, *Institutions for Effective Management of the Environment,* Part I (60002), 37 pp. National Academy of Sciences, Jan 70. Includes recommendations for an Analytical Environmental Institute modeled on the RAND Corp, a problem-oriented university, an environmental monitoring agency, a National Laboratory for Environmental Science, and federal government reorganization. Available from the National Academy of Sciences, 2101 Constitution Ave. N.W., Washington, D.C. 20418.

Proposal: National Institute of Ecology.
Ecological Society of America "National Institute of Ecology; An Operational Plan" (60003) 26 pp. Prepared by Peat, Marwick, Mitchell & Co., Dec 70. Available from Ecological Society of America, c/o Dr. William A. Niering, Secretary Connecticut College, New London, Conn. 06320.

National Centers for Environmental Research.
U.S Senate, Committee on Public Works, "The Case for National Environmental Laboratories" (60004) Committee Print, Jan 70 (91st Congress, 2d Session) of report of Ad Hoc NEL Concept Committee of the Oak Ridge National Laboratory.

Missed Institutional Opportunities in Environmental Studies.
Philip C. Ritterbush, "Environmental Studies: The Search for an Institutional Form" (60005) *Minerva*, Vol. 9 (1971), pp. 493-509. Describes a number of current proposals for the development of environmental research institutions, including the National Institute of Ecology, the Oak Ridge National Laboratory Environmental Program, the analytic institute proposed by the National Academy of Sciences and President Nixon, national environmental laboratories, and university centers. Includes an historical sketch of human ecology, with numerous references, arguing that institutions failed to establish adequate research programs in the 1920's, when the field was ripe for expansion, because they were too committed to disciplinary departmental structures.

Regional Ecological Knowledge and Advisory Centers.
William R. Ewald, Jr., 1150 Connecticut Avenue, N.W., Washington, D.C. 20036, "Managing the Environment Now for the World Ahead" (60006), 49 pp., 18 Jan 72. The author, a planner and development consultant, believes that universities must invariably fail to provide interdisciplinary contexts to which faculty members would subordinate their professional independence and claims for recognition. Funding for such centers would be very difficult to secure and their findings might be disregarded by major social institutions. He therefore proposes that regional electric utilities provide funding for long-range resource policy planning as an overhead on energy costs, to be supplemented by government and other research support. The paper proposes a "social invention": regional ecological knowledge and advisory centers, operating independently of government and industry. He concludes with a description of Santa Barbara as a model setting for such a center. His proposal that resource research be made part of the rate base of utilities deserves wide consideration.

International Institute for Environmental Affairs.
A service organization under the auspices of the Aspen Institute for Humanistic Studies, 600 Fifth Ave., New York, New York 10020. Jack Raymond, President. Documents include Thomas W. Wilson, Jr., "The Environment: Too Small a View," an Occasional Paper of the Aspen Institute (1970), 32 pp. (6.10020)

Cooperative Science Education Center.
156 Adams Lane, Oak Ridge, Tenn. 37830. Program documents on citizen and student involvement in technology assessment, including "A Proposal for the Establishment of an Institute for Environmental Problem Assissment Education," 48 pp.; "ENVIRO COUNTY," designs for simulations of environmental policy-making; and monthly newsletters. (6.37830)

Federal Environmental Research.
Oak Ridge National Laboratory, *The Environmental and Technology Assessment Progress Report, June-December 1970* (Feb 71), 254 pp. No. ORNL NSF-EP-3. Limited number of copies available on request from Dr. J.H. Gibbons, Director, ORNL-NSF Environmental Program, Oak Ridge National Laboratory, Oak Ridge, Tenn. 37830. The first section, previously issued as ORNL 4632, is a report by David Rose, who served as director of a summer project to develop proposals for ORNL involvement in environmental studies, relating how new options for the institutions were identified and evaluated. The second section describes subsequent progress in seven core areas of the environmental research program being developed: Program Perception and Planning, Material Resources and Recycle, Electrical Energy and Its Environmental Impact, Environmental Information System, Regional Modeling, Environmental Indices, and Education/Communication. The third section gives a brief summary of major research efforts already underway on materials in streams, environmental mutagenesis, and the mutation rate in man. A revealing and significant account of the major changes in program direction in one of the nation's major research institutions. (6.37830)

7. Governing, Public Policy

NIXON AND AGNEW

Common Cause.
Report from Washington and other documents (7000). Issued ten times yearly. Memberships from $15.00 per year. 2100 M St., N.W., Washington, D.C. 20037; Common Cause is the citizen's lobby headed by former Secretary of Health, Education, and Welfare John Gardner.

The Public Policy Role of Nonprofit Institutions.
U.S. Senator Edmund S. Muskie, Remarks on introduction and text of legislation to free nonprofit institutions from prohibitions against lobbying (7001), *Congressional Record,* 24 Jan 72, S287-295. Accompanied by a paper by Theodore L. Garrett, "Federal Tax Limitations on Political Activities of Public Interest and Educational Organizations."

Technology Assessment and Public Policy.
Science Policy Research Division, U.S. Congressional Research Service, for the Subcommittee on Science, Research, and Development, Committee on Science and Astronautics, U.S. House of Representatives, 92nd Congress, 1st Session, Committee Print, Serial A, *Technical Information for Congress* (7002) 15 April 71, xxiii, 845 pp. This formidable compendium offers eighteen case studies on technical issues considered by the Congress, along with a bibliography on technical assessment. It portrays in depth the kinds of challenges posed to the policy process by science and technology. Among the case studies are "Congressional Response to Project Camelot," pp. 126-160, "High-Energy Physics, an Issue without a Focus," pp. 263-287, and "A Technology Assessment of the Vietnam Defoliant Matter: An Evaluation by a Scientific Organization," pp. 531-590.

Public Interest Movement in the Professions.
Documents are sought for a collection on concepts of social responsibility in the academic and learned professions, e.g. Robert Reinhold, "Young Professionals Turning Activist," *The New York Times,* 11 Jan 71. (7003)

The Center Magazine.
Center for the Study of Democratic Institutions, bimonthly for members, annual dues $15.00. Editor, John Cogley. From the Center, Box 4068, Santa Barbara, California 93103. (7004)

A Revealing Controversy over Scientific Advice.
The Archives of Institutional Change invites submissions of documents on the report of the Operations Research Society of America, "Guidelines for the Practice of Operations Research," *Operations Research,* Vol. 19, no. 5 (Sept 71), and replies by ABM opponents who were criticized in the report. (7005)

GOVERNMENTAL AND CIVIC INSTITUTIONS

U.S. Civil Service Commission.
Samuel Stafford, "Civil Service Commission Is Achieving Responsiveness" (70000) *Government Executive,* Feb 71. Reprinted in the *Congressional Record* for 23 Feb 71, pp. E1099-1100.

Proposal for New Social Research Agency.
National Academy of Sciences, "Behavioral and Social Research in the Department of Defense: A Framework for Management" (70001). (1971) 55 pp., $2.25 from the Publications Office, 2101 Constitution Ave. N.W., Washington, D.C. 20418. Proposal for a new governmental institution to conduct overseas social science research sponsored by national security agencies.

Executive Development for Public Service.
Ward Stewart and John C. Honey, *University-Sponsored Executive Development Programs in the Public Service* (70002) (U.S. Office of Education, 1966), 82 pp. incl. bibliography. Describes 24 university-based programs for mid-career executive development, a type of program likely to be expanded under the new Intergovernmental Personnel Act of 1971.

Institutional Change Design for Political Party.
Commission on Party Structure and Delegate Selection, Democratic National Committee, "Mandate for Reform. . ." (70003), *Congressional Record,* 22 Sept 71, E9841-855.

Public Interest Research Group.
1025 15th Street, N.W., Washington, D.C. 20005. Established by Ralph Nader to perform policy research and foster the extension of public interest advocacy nationwide. One of its efforts is to secure support from student activity funds for the establishment of public interest research groups at the state level. Other documents include a Property Tax Newsletter and the Public Interest Press Service. (7.20005)

Social Statistics—Politicization of Institutions.
Criticisms of changes in the U.S. Bureau of Labor Statistics apparently reflecting political pressures to interpret unemployment and employment statistics so as to favor the position of the Nixon Administration, including a letter of protest from eleven members of the Economics Department at Michigan State University. *Congressional Record,* 12 Oct 71, S16183-84, and 23 Nov 71, S19435-36. (7.20210)

The Adlai Stevenson Institute.
5757 South Woodlawn Avenue, Chicago, Illinois 60637. "Current programs seek better, cheaper, more humane approaches to problems in the neighborhoods of Chicago and cities in Africa and Asia; to violence on the streets of America and both in and among other countries; to the needs and dilemmas of education and to the environmental problems which loom so menacingly over the whole planet." Headquarters in the famed Robie House designed by Frank Lloyd Wright. Brochure (7.60637).

8. Science

THE TOWER OF BABEL

Criticism of National Academy of Sciences.
Stewart Udall, "Science in Ferment" (8000), *Newsday,* 9-10 Jan 71.

Organization of Government Research Programs.
Jerome B. Wiesner, "Rethinking Our Scientific Objectives" (8001), *Technology Review,* Vol. 71 (Jan 69), pp. 15-17. Dr. Wiesner calls for purposeful expansion of the National Science Foundation in order "to reorganize and strengthen the federal mechanisms for planning and supporting research and development."

Organization of Government Research Support.
Herbert Roback, "Do We Need a Department of Science and Technology?" (8002), *Science,* Vol. 169 (4 Jul 71) pp. 36-43.

Proposed Centralization of Government Research.
U.S. House of Representatives, Committee on Science and Astronautics, "The National Institutes of Research and Advanced Studies: A Recommendation for Centralization of Federal Responsibilities" (8003), Apr 70, 32 pp. A report of the Committee's Subcommittee on Science, Research, and Development.

Budget Cuts Prompt Examination of Policy.
John Walsh "Science Policy: Budget Cuts Prompt Closer Look at the System" (8004), *Science,* Vol. 168 (15 May 70), pp. 802-5.

Institutional Consequences of Military-Sponsored Research.
Princeton University Special Committee on Sponsored Research, *Report to the Council of the Princeton University Community.* 86 pp. (8005) The Special Committee. chaired by physicist Thomas S. Kuhn, decided that, for the most part, ". . .existing policies and procedures are adequate to prohibit individually unsuitable projects. . ." They then addressed themselves to the question, "Has the University. . .developed adequate techniques for the preservation of the independence on which its integrity depends?" They offered no answers in the preliminary report, but concluded *"that the problems inherent in the present system of federal support urgently need more study."* (emphasis in original, p. 15)

Science Policy.
(8006) Science Policy Foundation, monthly. 36 Craven Street, London WCZN 5NG, England. Published in collaboration with the Organisation for Economic Cooperation and Development. Maurice Goldsmith, Editor. Annual subscription L 9.00 airmail to individuals, L11.00 to institutions.

Newsletter on Science and Public Affairs.
Federation of American Scientists, Jeremy J. Stone, Director, *F.A.S. Newsletter* (8007). Issued ten times yearly. Membership, $7.50 for students, from $15.00 for others; 203 C St. N.E., Washington, D.C. 20002.

Science and Public Policy Study Group.
Newsletter (8008) Issued ten times yearly. Howard J. Lewis, Editor. Annual sub-

scription, $15.00, individuals; $30.00, institutions. MIT Press, 28 Carleton Street, Cambridge, Mass. 02142.

Recommendations for a National Science Policy.
U.S. House of Representatives, Committee on Science and Astronautics, "Toward a Science Policy for the United States." (8009), Committee Print, 15 Oct 70 (91st Congress, 2nd Session), 62 pp. This report of the Subcommittee on Science, Research, and Development urges the formulation of explicit national policies to promote optimal development of science and technology. Among the institutional aspects of the recommendations were reiterated support for a system of direct institutional grants, endorsement of proposals to create inter-disciplinary problem-solving institutions independent of the universities, affirmation of support of academic science by mission-oriented agencies, and continued reliance on the universities for leadership in basic research.

Physics: A Look beyond the Funding Crisis.
Raymond Bowers, "Some Views on Physics and Society" (8010), *American Scientist,* Vol. 58 (Nov/Dec 70), pp. 607-611.

Science and Public Understanding.
Scientists' Institute for Public Information, *S.I.P.I. Report* (8011) Issued four times yearly by the Institute (Margaret Mead, President; Barry Commoner, Chairman). Membership, from $25.00; 30 East 68th St., New York, New York 10021.

Institutional Support.
U.S. House of Representatives, Committee on Science and Astronautics, *Hearings on Institutional Grants Legislation,* (8012) 1968 (90th Cong., 2d Session) and 1969 (91st Cong., 1st Session). Two vols., iv + 388 pp. and iv + 351 pp. Hearings of the Subcommittee on Science, Research, and Development.

Cultural Relations of Science.
M. Neville McMorris, "Historical Perspectives on the Two-Culture Debate" (8013), *Main Currents in Modern Thought,* Vol. 27 (Mar-Apr 71), pp. 103-112. Interpretation of the two-culture debate in light of the history of concepts of culture in relation to science. Urges "the recognition and the acceptance of the complementary nature of both instruments, operating within the same domain of culture." The author is Professor of Physics, University of West Indies, Kingston, Jamaica.

Newsletter on Science Politics.
Daniel Greenberg, ed., *Science and Government Report* (8014), $25.00 per year, P.O. Box 21123, Washington, D.C. 20009. Reprints of first year available.

Scientists and Social Policy.
Martin Brown, ed., *The Social Responsibility of the Scientist* (8015) (New York:

Free Press, 1971) 282 pp. $3.95. Sixteen lectures in a course offered at Berkeley in the spring of 1969, these essays explore the interactions of professional values, scientific societies, government patronage, and universities. Highly suitable for instructional use.

Science in Culture.

Thomas R. Blackburn. "Sensuous-Intellectual Complementarity in Science; counter-cultural epistemology has something of value to contribute to the science of complex systems" (8016), *Science,* Vol. 172 (4 June 71), pp. 1003-7. Changing character of modern science and its implications for the practice of research and undergraduate education. Need for receptivity within science to intuitive and "sensuous" insights, which are complementary to rather than contradictory of quantitative expressions of rationality. The author is Associate Professor of Chemistry at Hobart and William Smith Colleges.

The Career of Reason.

Rene Dubos, *Reason Awake: Science for Man* (8017) (New York: Columbia University Press, 1970) xix + 280 pp., paper, $2.95. Dubos castigates the conventional view that science develops autonomously, uninfluenced by social needs, and that the growth of knowledge cannot be planned. The changing emphasis of biomedical research institutions from microbiology to biochemistry to genetics to behavioral research "has a logic which is not inherent in science itself, but is derived from social concerns." Dubos persuasively argues that social forces bring about significant shifts in the directions of scientific research and views conventional academic organization, when it resists such currents, as a serious obstacle to social improvement. These considerations lead him to espouse the creation of special research institutes oriented toward social purposes, whose operation would also entail efforts to educate the wider public about science and technology. Conscious efforts to shape the research enterprise might regain for man the capacity to influence his future.

International Science Policy.

U.S. House of Representatives, Committee on Foreign Affairs, "Science, Technology, and American Diplomacy" (8018) Committee Print, May 70, 91st Congress, 2d Session, 40 pp. Bibliography issued by the Subcommittee on National Security Policy and Scientific Developments.

Reorientation of Scientific Research toward Social Needs.

The Archives of Institutional Change issues a standing invitation for documents and reprints on this subject. (8019)

Role of Scientists in Public Policy.

Dean Schooler, Jr., *Science, Scientists, and Public Policy* (8020) (New York: The Free Press, 1971; xiv + 338 pp., $6.95. Areas of public policy rated according to degree of influence by scientists in the postwar period.

Socially Concerned Scientists.
Victor Cohn, "Scientists Face Their Frankensteins" (8021), *Washington Post,* Section H, 27 June 71. Report on Scientists and Engineers for Social and Political Action (SESPA).

Science Policy Reviews.
Battelle Memorial Institute, (8022) published quarterly by the Institute, 505 King Ave., Columbus, Ohio 43201. Formerly *Science Policy Bulletin.* Abstracts mainly of articles on national programs and policies in science and technology. Little coverage of institutions. Clyde Tipton, Editor.

Call for End to Mission-Oriented Research Support.
Jacob Bronowski, "The Disestablishment of Science" (8023), *Encounter* Vol. 36, No. 7 (Jul 71). Argues that scientists should assume direct control of the disbursement of public funds for research in order to preserve the integrity of knowledge from the interests of government agencies.

Human Adaptability.
Van Rensselaer Potter, "Society and Science" (8024), *Science,* Vol. 146 (20 Nov 64), pp. 1018-22. A key concept in biology applied to society.

Science and Social Ethics.
Van Rensselaer Potter, "Bridge to the Future: The Concept of Human Progress" (8025), *Land Economics,* Vol. 38, No. 1 (Feb 62), pp. 1-8.

Bibliography on Science and Public Policy.
Lynton K. Caldwell, ed., *Science, Technology, and Public Policy* (8026) Two volumes, 1968, 555 pp. Available from the Department of Government, Indiana University, Bloomington, Indiana 47401. Vol. I, Bibliography, 492 pp., includes a short section on institutions, pp. 269-283. Vol. II, Syllabus for Advanced Study.

Science Studies.
(8027) Published quarterly. Subscriptions, $12.50, U.S.A.; $13.50, Canada; Five pounds elsewhere, from Macmillan Journals Ltd., Subscription Dept., Brunel Road, Basingstoke, Hampshire, England. Editors: Roy MacLeod, Science Policy Unit, University of Sussex; and David Edge, Science Studies Unit, University of Edinburgh. Research in the social and historical dimensions of science and technology.

Scientists and Engineers for Social and Political Action.
Science for the People (8028). Bimonthly, each issue edited by an ad hoc collective. Regular memberships, $10.00. 9 Walden Street, Jamaica Plain, Mass. 02130.

Congressional Appraisal of Social Aspects of Science.
U.S. House of Representatives, Committee on Science and Astronautics. Sub-

committee on Science, Research, and Development, *Government and Science* (8029), a series of five reports issued as Committee Prints, 1963-65, in an effort to delineate a legislative context for science policy issues. 258 pp. (88th and 89th Congresses).

Impact of Science on Society.
(8030) Editor in Chief, Bruno Friedman, United Nations Scientific and Cultural rganization, Place de Fontenoy, 75 Paris VII, France. Quarterly, subscriptions $4.00 from Box 433, New York, New York 10016.

Science and Social Interests.
American Association for the Advancement of Science, *Science for Society; A Bibliography, 3rd ed.* (8031) from the Association, 1515 Massachusetts Avenue, N.W., Washington, D.C. 20005, xi + 92 pp. For secondary school and introductory college use. Prepared by Howard T. Bausum.

The Life Sciences and Social Interests: An Overview.
Philip Handler, ed., *Biology and the Future of Man* (8032) (Oxford University Press, 1970) xxiv, 967 pp. $4.95 paper. This splendid volume was written by a group of leading biologists in an effort to describe the present state of knowledge in relation to the interests of man and society. In order to address the vast range of concerns of the life sciences it had to become almost epic in scope. The authors offer the first summary interpretation of a field of current science that may also fairly be considered a commentary on its social relevance. While they do not address recommendations to institutions for implementation, their appraisal of human interests as affected by all the major fields of biology makes the report a richly useful general reference likely to be of lasting value as a background to institutional policy and planning.

Proposal: A Guild of Scientists.
Henry W. Menard, *Science: Growth and Change* (8033) (Harvard University Press, 1971) xii + 216 pp., $10.00. A general union of scientists and technologists is suggested in order to limit the labor supply and eliminate unemployment, monitor immigration and Ph.D. output, and represent the social interests of members.

R&D Management Digest.
(8034) Editor, Lowell Hattery. Monthly, subscriptions $24.00 from Lomond Systems, Inc., Mt. Airy, Maryland 21771.

First General Congressional Review of Science and Society.
U.S. House of Representatives, Select Committee on Government Research, *Studies and Hearings* (8035) 13 items, 1963-1964 (88th Congress).

Scientific Institutions and Social Purpose.
Sir Gordon Sutherland, "The Organization and Financing of Research both Na-

tionally and Internationally" (8036), *Bulletin of the Institute of Physics and the Physical Society,* Aug 66, pp. 262-275.

The Organization of Scientific Functions.
Frank E. Hartung, "Science as an Institution" (8037), *Philosophy of Science,* Vol. 18 (1951), pp. 35-54.

Organization of Sponsored Resarch.
Lord Rothschild and Frederick Dainton, *A Framework for Government Research and Development* (8038). Cmnd. 4814. London: H.M. Stationery Office, 1971; reprinted, 1972. i, 43 pp. 52.5 pence; 49 High Holborn, London WC1V 6HB. Lord Rothschild is Head of the Central Policy Review Staff of the British Government. His recommenuation that government departments control research sponsored in their areas of program responsibility by the Research Councils, heretofore independent of them, has touched off a storm of protest by the Royal Society and many other elements of the British scientific community. In his devotion to the idea that applied research should have a "customer," which he considers to be a government department serving a particular function, he has neglected a host of more subtle linkages between the directions of applied research and components of the institutional system other than national government. The Rothschild recommendations reflect the growing tendency to seek immediate "payoffs" from research rather than patiently seek out institutional deficiencies and correct them where they occur. Sir Frederick Dainton's working group submitted a report, "The Future of the Research Council System," recommending improved coordination of the councils through a Board of the Research Councils succeeding the existing Council for Scientific Policy.

A Representative Reaction to Defense R&D.
U.S. Senator Tom McIntyre, "Defense Research and Development— Some Observations" (8039), *Congressional Record,* 9 Dec 71, S21037-40. The chairman of the Ad Hoc Subcommittee on Research and Development of the Senate Armed Services Committee discusses needs for management improvement in military R&D, the uncertain future of contract research centers, Soviet technology, and public attitudes toward the military, in a revised version of comments prepared for the Defense Science Board.

Science and Society: Too Many Imponderables?
Harvey Brooks, "Can Science Survive in the Modern Age?" (8040) , *Science,* Vol. 174 (1 Oct 71), pp. 21-30. How does science respond to the external demands of society? "Like an organism responding to disease . . ."? By "natural selection of ideas"? By becoming "contaminated . . . with the militaristic, materialistic, and selfish features of the popular

culture"? By becoming "inherently biased by the sociopolitical environment in which it is embedded"? By "a natural swing of the pendulum away from what was, perhaps, an overemphasis on the cognitive aspects of human personality"? By a defeatist sense that the edifice of knowledge is complete in outline and that no fundamental new ideas will arise? Brooks is sure that science will change, but he seems overwhelmed by all the alternatives he has identified. He entirely fails to consider how the institutional system of science regulates and mediates its interactions with social processes and cultural trends, and thus confesses that he has no certain sense of where science may be tending. This is a stunning confession from the Dean of the Division of Engineering and Applied Physics at Harvard, who for twenty years has played a prominent role in what passes for a national science policy process. It shows how weak and uncertain conventional thinking about science in relation to society has been. Their interactions simply occur, "out there," somewhere, somehow, in a structureless gaseous swirl, a plenum whose tendencies are unknowable and which will therefore forever take us by surprise. The need for analysis of the institutional processes involved in the social relations of science becomes insistently clear from Dean Brooks' failure to formulate a strategy for inquiry that could encompass social policies to sustain science in facing its uncertain future.

Science, the Demand for Applications.
John Walsh, "National Science Foundation: Managing Applied Research" (8041) , *Science,* Vol. 175 (11 Feb 72), pp. 611-614. Despite university apprehension the National Science Foundation is expanding its RANN (Research Applied to National Needs) Program, in response to public and Congressional appetite for applications of scientific knowledge.

Institutions Restricting the Scope of Professional Ethics.
Ralph Nader, "The Scientist and His Indentured Professional Societies" (8042) , *Bulletin of the Atomic Scientists,* Feb 72, pp. 43-46. Scientific societies tend to be indentured to the industries they serve, and thus do not afford protection to members seeking to exercise professional ethics. Thus the American Institute of Industrial Engineers refused a request for support from A. Ernest Fitzgerald, who lost his job as a result of his effort to expose cost overruns in procurement for the Air Force C5-A transport. Nader argues that such societies should "stake out their readiness to defend their colleagues when they are arbitrarily treated for activity in which they were involved." (p. 46)

Universities and the Urban Poor.
Organization for Social and Technical Innovation (8043), U.S. Office of Education 50062, *Urban Universities: Rhetoric, Reality, and Conflict*

(Washington: U.S. Government Printing Office, June 70), vi, 65 pp., $0.65. Emphasizes barriers to communication and coincidence of view

Science and Social Interests.
William Bevan, "The General Scientific Association: A Bridge to Society at Large" (8044) , *Science,* Vol. 172 (23 April 71), pp. 349-352. Describes a profusion of activities undertaken by the American Association for the Advancement of Science in hopes of fostering a response to social interests on the part of the scientific community, with strong emphasis on widening public understanding of science.

Mismanagement of Government Research Support.
Senator Edmund S. Muskie, "The Crisis in Academic Research" (8045), *Congressional Record,* 6 Aug 71, S13454-56. Describes unexpected cancellations of research support and inconsistencies of approach among funding agencies that have devastating consequences at the level of the single institution.

Institutional Impact of Research Funding Shifts.
Thomas J. Kennedy, Jr., John F. Sherman, and R. W. Lamont-Havers, "Factors Contributing to Current Distress in the Academic Community" (8046), *Science,* 11 Feb 72, pp. 599-607. Institutional research capability has declined more rapidly than level funding totals might indicate between 1967 and 1970, largely because of increases in investigators' salaries, according to this analysis by senior officers of the extramural program of the National Institutes of Health.
of Health.

Need for Government Leadership in Strengthening Science.
Subcommittee on Science, Research, and Development, Committee on Science and Astronautics, U.S. House of Representatives, 91st Congress, 2nd Session, *Toward a Science Policy for the United States* (8047), Committee Print (115 pp.) and Hearings (936 pp.), 1970.

SCIENTIFIC INSTITUTIONS

Governing Values in Science Grounded in Community.
Norman W. Storer, *The Social System of Science* (80000) (N.Y.: Holt, Rinehart and Winston, 1966) vi + 180 pp., $4.15. Regards the three central values of scientific research as disinterestedness of individuals, organized scepticism, and communality—which are maintained by collective responses. It is their capacity to mediate such collective responses that makes scientific institutions so important.

Scientific Institution-Building, a Social History.
Howard S. Miller, *Dollars for Research: Science and Its Patrons in Nineteenth-Century America* (80001) (University of Washington Press, 1970) xii + 258 pp., $9.50.

The Federal Government Research Establishment.
U.S. House of Representatives, Committee on Science and Astronautics, Subcommittee on Science, Research, and Development, *Utilization of Federal Laboratories, Hearings* (80002) (March and April, 1968, 457 pp. The Federal Government owns and operates over 100 major laboratories without effective central coordination or review. One study by the (then) Science Biology Research Division of the Legislative Reference Service, for the Research and Technical Programs Subcommittee of the House Committee on Government Operations, *A Case Study of the Utilization of Federal Laboratory Resources* (89th Congress, 2d Session, Nov 66), 140 pp. (80003), found that almost two hundred government laboratories were doing pollution studies. There has since been no answer to their question, "Should a consistent and comprehensive Federal policy covering the performance of research and development, the utilization of laboratory resources, the relationship to the private sector, and the creation of new resources be separately formulated and formally issued?" (p. 60)

Alternatives to Academic Science.
Michael J. Moravcsik, "Reflections on National Laboratories" (80004), *Bulletin of the Atomic Scientists,* Feb 70, pp. 11-16.

Science outside the Academic Setting.
Victor J. Danilov, "The Not-for-Profit Research Institutes" (80005), *Industrial Research,* Feb 66, pp. 29-39.

Institutional Influences on Scientific Development.
Charles E. Rosenberg, "Factors in the Development of Genetics in the United States: Some Suggestions" (80006), *Journal of the History of Medicine and Allied Sciences,* Vol. 22 (1967), pp. 27-46. Comparison of the response of three institutional systems—agriculture, medicine, and universities—to research opportunities in genetics. "Each of the potential research contexts we have discussed— agricultural institutions, medicine, the universities—provided a quite different scientific environment. Each presented a characteristic texture, a mosaic of the social, economic, and institutional factors which ordered the roles and expectations of the men functioning within them." (p. 45)

Systems Design, the Prerequisite for Institutional Success.
Boyd R. Keenan, "The Search for an Institutional System for Science" (80007), introduction to *Science and the University* (Columbia University Press, 1966), pp. 1-12. Argues that "the construction of an institutional system for science" is a leading intellectual task faced by all those concerned about the future development of society. "The American scientific edifice is a monument to many dedicated scientists and public servants. But none can deny that it is also the product of a multiplicity of unconnected crash programs, haphazard coordination, and plain political accidents." (p. 4)

Planning a System of Scientific Institutions.
Joint Committee on Atomic Energy, 86th Congress, 2nd Session, *The Future*

Role of the Atomic Energy Commission Laboratories (80008) Committee Print (U.S.G.P.O., 1960), 277 pp. A report by the AEC and replies by industry, educational institutions, the laboratories themselves, and other interested groups.

The Morning of America's Scientific Institutions.
Bernard Jaffe, *Outposts of Science; A Journey to the Workshops of Our Leading Men of Research* (80009) (N.Y.: Simon and Schuster, 1935) xxvi + 546 pp.

Hybrid Research Establishments in Flux.
Dean C. Coddington and J. Gordon Milliken, "Future of Federal Contract Research Centers" (80010), *Harvard Business Review,* Mar-Apr 70, pp. 103-116. Argues that contract research centers do best when carrying out the mission of a sponsor, whether a government agency or local government, but that they should not be permitted to become multi-purpose diversified establishments performing on behalf of many interests.

Institutional Involvement in Military Research.
Dorothy Nelkin, "The Science, Technology, and Society Series," *The University and Military Research; Moral Politics at M.I.T.* (8.02139) (Cornell University Press, 1972) xi + 195 pp., $1.95. The decision to divorce the Instrumentation Laboratory from MIT did not resolve genuine conflicts between the external social aims which contending factions urge the university to serve.

Woods Hole Oceanographic Institution.
Woods Hole, Massachusetts 02543, *Forty Years of Research and Education* (1970), 88 pp. (8.02543)

Pursuit.
Quarterly journal of the Society for the Investigation of the Unexplained. (8.07832) Editor, Hans Stefan Santesson. Annual subscription, $5.00 from the Society, Columbia, New Jersey 07832. Field investigations of scientific mysteries.

Institute for the Study of Science in Human Affairs.
Columbia University, New York, New York 10027. Bibliographies, occasional papers, and a rationale for the program (discontinued in 1972) by Christopher Wright, Director. (8.10027)

Program on Science, Technology, and Society.
Cornell University (8.14850), Program Description and Course List, 1970-71, 13 pp. Available from the Program, 632 Clark Hall, Cornell University, Ithaca, New York 14850.

Society for Social Responsibility in Science.
A membership organization formed in 1949, devoted to fostering a sense of personal moral responsibility among scientists. Annual dues: sustaining, $25.00; regular, $10.00; others keyed to income. Publishes a *Newsletter,* 221 Rock Hill Road, Bala-Cynwyd, Pennsylvania (8.19004)

American Association for the Advancement of Science.
Philip Boffey, three articles, *Science,* Vol. 172 (30 Apr 71) pp. 453-58; (7 May 71) pp. 542-47; (14 May 71) pp. 656-68. Critique of new roles and plans for expansion. (8.20005)

Policy Studies in Science and Technology.
George Washington University, Program of Policy Studies in Science and Technology (8.20006), Publications list, program brochure, and 1969-70 report; Available from the Program of Policy Studies, George Washington University, Room 800, 2100 Pennsylvania Ave., Washington, D.C. 20006.

Strengthening the Institutional Framework for Science Policy.
Robert Lamson, Science Policy Research Section, Social Science Division, National Science Foundation, Washington, D.C. 20550, Science Policy — Needed Actions and Institutions" (8.20550) 10 Jan 72, 6 pp. Discusses needs for an annual report on science and technology, policy research, and an information system. Also "Needed Research for Science Policy" 20 pp.

Science, Statistical Measures, Bibliography
Division of Science Resources and Policy Studies, *Publications* (8.20550). National Science Foundation, Washington, D.C. 20550, Dec 1970, 18 pp. and supplement.

University Science Planning and Policy Program,
National Science Foundation, Washington, D.C. 20550. Summaries of objectives and activities supported. (8.20550)

Center for Research on Utilization of Scientific Knowledge
Institute for Social Research, University of Michigan, Ann Arbor, Michigan 48104. Studies the processes required for the full use of research findings and new knowledge. (8.48104)

Council for Biology in Human Affairs.
(8.92112) Sponsored by the Salk Institute. "Typical Examples of Work of the Council for Biology in Human Affairs" Jul 71, 78 pp. Discussions of gene therapy, mood-altering drugs, and urban ecology. Other papers from the Salk Institute, including "Basic Background on Scientific Research at the Salk Institute."

Institutional Impact of Military Research Support.
Stanford Workshop on Political and Social Issues, Room 590A Old Union, Stanford University, Stanford, Calif. 94305, *DOD Sponsored Research at Stanford* (8.94305). 2 vols. 338 + 117 pp. Extensive compilation on DOD-funded research at Stanford University, which documents differences between project descriptions written by military research agencies to justify support of the work and project descriptions written by the investigators themselves.

9. Culture, Art, Religion, Philosophy

CORNELL

The Future of Institutions: Conjecture and Response.
Robert Theobald and J.M. Scott, *Teg's 1994; An Anticipation of the Near Future* (9000) ı (Chicago: Swallow Press, 1972) xix, 211 pp. $2.50. Spurning the convention whereby futurists have sought to extrapolate the present into the future, the economist Robert Theobald and his anthropologist wife extend this invitation to readers to participate in shaping the future by commenting upon and modifying their sketch of a special learning and communications center for highly gifted young people in 1994. The Orwell Foundation, created in 1984 by a group of liberal humanists to foster world citizenship has aided the formation of communication processes through which aspirant creators of ideas acknowledge a duty to receive and respond to the ideas of others. Such a commitment is intended to achieve a more rapid rate of change in ideas, which the authors believe necessary for the creation of a new culture. "The task we must carry through in the immediate future is therefore totally different from that which our present institutions were designed to accomplish. Until we began to perceive the need for a profound shift in idea-structures, we were properly occupied as individuals and nations with the fulfillment of already-known goals. Now that we are becoming aware that we must change our idea-structures, and with them our processes, we are confronted with a different challenge. The challenge is to create a different pattern of societal organization: in effect, a new culture." (p. xiii) No arguments are offered for the proposition that the rate of change in thought can be accelerated through saturation communication, nor for the assumption that such change is culturally beneficial. The book includes plans for a "multihogan" complex where "communications carrels" and other technological resources would be available — an electronic commune with a self-conscious debt to Navajo settlement patterns, for which a floor plan is offered.

Demonstration to Promote Environmental Consciousness.
Robert Atkinson, "Clearwater: Sloop and Goal" *Museum News,* Vo. 49, No. 2 (Oct 70) pp. 21-24. Describes Pete Seeger's efforts to interest Hudson River Valley residents in environmental preservation by building a sloop as a focus for a revival of historical and ecological consciousness. "There may be no better way of learning about the past than by participating in and reliving it. . . . Existing museums—and hopefully groups—can learn from what the Hudson River Sloop Restoration is doing and do it themselves."

Humanities Education.
The Humanities Journal (9002) Publication of the National Asssociation for Humanities Education. Five times yearly. Annual subscription, $10.00. Editor, Herbert Safran. A medium for exchange of ideas about humanities education from school through college. Vol. 4, No. 3 (May 71) contains a list of 153 colleges and universities with interdisciplinary arts and humanities programs. P.O. Box 628, Kirksville, Mo. 63401.

Wider Significances for Literary Studies.
Maynard Mack, "To See It Feelingly" (9003), *PMLA, Publications of the Modern Language Association of America,* Vol. 86, no. 3 (May 71), pp. 363-374.

Federal Funds for Preservation of Folk and Popular Culture.
Senator Fred Harris, Remarks on introduction and text of S.1930 (9004), *Congressional Record,* 24 May 71, 4 pp. S.1930 would create an American Folklife Foundation in the Library of Congress.

Experiments in Art and Technology.
Calvin Tompkins, "E.A.T." (9005), *The New Yorker,* 3 Oct 70, pp. 83-133. Describes the presentation at the Osaka Exposition by Experiments in Art and Technology.

Protecting Majority Cultural Values from Challenge.
Federal Communications Commissioner Nicholas Johnson, Dissenting Statement (9006) FCC 71-205 (5 Mar 71), 17 pp. Dissent from ruling by the Commission that broadcast stations must screen song lyrics for references to illegal drugs. Johnson charges that the real target of the Commission's majority was cultural experimentation, not the social harm caused by drug abuse.

Arts in Society.
(9007) Published three times per year. Subscriptions, $5.50 per year; students, $5.00, from Arts in Society, University Extension, University of Wisconsin, 606 State St., Madison, Wis. 53706. Explores the relationship of the arts to the institutions of society.

The Journal of Aesthetic Education.
(9008) Published quarterly. Subscriptions, $7.50, domestic; $8.00 foreign. University of Illinois Press, Urbana, Illinois 61801. Editor: Ralph A. Smith, Associate Professor of Aesthetic Education, University of Illinois. The *Journal* seeks an understanding of education in the arts and humanities, aesthetic aspects of the art and craft of teaching, appreciation of the aesthetic character of other disciplines, new communications media, and environmental arts. "The major purpose of the *Journal* is to clarify the issues of aesthetic education understood in its most extensive meaning, including not only the problems of formal instruction in the arts and humanities at all levels of schooling, but also the aesthetic problems of the larger society created by twentieth-century existence."

Journal of Popular Culture.
(9009) Published quarterly. Subscriptions, $8.00; $4.00 for students. Editorial and subscription correspondence: Ray B. Browne, University Hall, Bowling Green University, Bowling, Green, Ohio 43403.

Involvement of Art in Social Thought.
Donald D. Egbert, *Social Radicalism and the Arts; Western Europe. A Cultural*

History from the French Revolution to 1968 (9010) (New York: Alfred A. Knopf, 1970) xx + 821 pp. and 53 pp. index, illus., $15.00. This is the first of three volumes on Marxist thought and the arts. One may confidently expect that the study of art in relation to society will be aided hugely by Professor Egbert's work. This volume is encyclopedic in scope. Fifty pages are devoted to the lives and theories of Marx and Engels. William Morris, his disciples, and the garden city movement receive equivalent coverage. Of institutions, the most detailed history is that of the Bauhaus, but trends bearing upon institutions are related, including academicism, criticism, art education, and didacticism. The volume constitutes a useful summary of the movements, schools, and associations which were the primary framework for the arts from 1800 to the present. Recently the Guggenheim Museum became embroiled in controversy over a decision not to mount an exhibit by Hans Haacke of photographs of slum dwellings accompanied by the names and addresses of their owners. Meetings of the College Art Association and the American Association of Museums have been interrupted by social protests. The social involvements of the arts will increasingly subject art schools and galleries to unfamiliar political pressures. Professor Egbert's study is invaluable as a background reference to inform the understanding of members and officers in art galleries and similar institutions in facing a turbulent future.

Popular Culture.
Russel B. Nye, *The Unembarrassed Muse; The Popular Arts in America* (9011) (New York: The Dial Press, 1970) vii + 497 pp. illus. incl. bibliog., $12.50. The history of the popular arts in America offers valuable clues to the democratization of culture today, as well as to the future vitality one may expect for the adversary youth culture. The author is Professor of English at Michigan State University.

Institutions and Cultural Transformation.
B. Michael Frolic, "A Visit to Peking University—What the Cultural Revolution Was All About" (9012), *New York Times Magazine,* 24 Oct 71, p. 29ff.

Effect on the Arts of Penchant for Novelty.
Saul Bellow, "Culture Now: Some Animadversions, Some Laughs" (9013), *Modern Occasions,* Winter 71, pp. 162-178. Degradation of the arts in a society bent on amusement and too impatient to nourish exceptional accomplishment. Complicity of the universities: "the sanctuary, at times the hospital, of literature, painting, music, and theatre."

Institutionalization of Cultural Values.
Hugh Dalziel Duncan, *Culture and Democracy; The Struggle for Form in Society and Architecture in Chicago in the Middle West during the Life and Times of Louis H. Sullivan* (9014) (Totowa, N.J.: Bedminster Press, 1965) xxii + 616 pp., illus. A massive study of the influences which rendered the Chicago cultural climate of the 1890's inhospitable to the work of Louis Sullivan. Recounts Sullivan's prescient beliefs about the kinds of schooling that would ᵻfoster environmental appreciation and induce receptivity to aesthetic experience.

A National Platform for the Humanities.
National Endowment for the Humanities, press release on the Jefferson Lecture (9015), 28 Jun 71, 3 pp. The Jefferson Lecture, to be given each year first at Washington, D.C., and then in certain other cities, is intended to convey important humanistic insights to a wider public, in order "that living issues may be the test of humane learning." Nominations invited by the National Council on the Humanities. The lecturer for the spring of 1972 was Lionel Trilling. Each year's lecturer will receive an award and stipend of $10,000 to support his preparation of the lectures.

Cultural Affairs.
Associated Councils of the Arts, issued at intervals since 1967. (9016) 1564 Broadway, New York, New York 10036. Temporarily suspended in 1972.

Art and Techne.
Leonardo: International Journal of the Contemporary Artist (9017) Published quarterly, Subscriptions, $7.50, individual; $25.00, institutional. Pergamon Press, Maxwell House, Fairview Park, Elmsford, New York 10523. Founded and edited by Frank Malina. "It will reflect the developing world-wide impact of contemporary works of art on mankind on a planet made small by modern means of communication and transportation and where the diversity of community life is being given a unifying basis by the universality of scientific and technological achievements." Departments include articles by artists, general articles, notes, documents, terminology, books, international art-science news, and letters.

Cultural Criticism and Comment.
Modern Occasions (9018) Published Quarterly. Subscriptions, $5.00 domestic, $6.00 foreign. Subscription addresses: East Coast, Bernard BeBoer, 188 High St., Nutley, New Jersey 07110; West Coast, L-S Distributors, 1161 Post St., San Francisco, Calif. 94109. Philip Rahv, Editor.

Humanities and Integration of Knowledge.
James H. Stone, "A Review of Recent Writings on the Humanities: A Critical and Bibliographical Study" (9019) in Maxwell H. Goldberg, ed., *Needles, Burrs, and Bibliographies; Study Resources: Technological Change, Human Values, and the Humanities* (*Pennsylvania State University, Center for Continuing Liberal Education, 1969*). Lists 79 books and 220 articles.

Renewal of Civilization Depends on New View of the Future.
Fred L. Polak, *The Image of the Future* (9020), 2 vols. (Leyden: A. W. Sythoff and N.Y.: Oceana Publications, 1961) 456 + 376 pp. A far-reaching cultural and sociological analysis of conceptions of the future as they have influenced social progress. Polak considers the central weakness of western culture to be the space left by the collapse of Christian eschatology, and senses great urgency in the need to find comparable images of the future with which to replace it.

Institutions, Social Change, and the Career of Ideas.
Bertrand de Jouvenel, *The Art of Conjecture* (9021) (N.Y.: Basic Books, 1967)
xii + 307 pp. trans. Nikita Lary A literate and humane disquisition on forecasting, in which deJouvenel cautions against expectations of certainty but per-
suasively argues that social change becomes much more tolerable if it is situated
in a context of purposive thought.

Institutions and the Adventure of Thought.
Herman Hesse, *Das Glasperlenspiel* (9022), translated by Richard and Clara
Winston as *Magister Ludi* (N.Y.: Bantam Books, 1972), xvii + 520 pp., $1.50.
One of the ideals underlying man's search for knowledge is formal purity of
thought. Hesse devises an elaborate institutional metaphor for that pursuit,
and offers a sensitive account of its limitations, in what may be the greatest work
of fiction ever written about the life of the mind, its dependence upon institutions,
and its relations to culture and society.

Workbook for Futurists.
Robert Theobald, *Futures Conditional* (9023) , forthcoming from Bobbs-
Merrill in 1972. 270 pp. mimeo, incl. bibliog. An anthology of conjecture
inviting response by the reader, dedicated "to those who choose to cooperate in creating the better future which is within our grasp." Theobald
repudiates the "extrapolist" view that the present determines the future
and the "romantic" view that changing consciousness will transform
society without active effort by citizens. Part I suggests ways in which the
future may be seen, including science fiction stories. Part II offers an
initial selection of material about the future, for the reader to expand with
additional items. Part III sets out a number of ways in which the reader
can participate in imagining the future. Part IV provides tools and
resources to aid the process of invention, including a bibliography by
nation. Pre-publication copies available for $6.00 (30% less in quantities
of 5 or more) from Personalized Secretarial Service, 5309 North 7th Street,
Phoenix, Arizona 85014.

Critique of Forecasting.
Robert Nisbet, "Has Futurology a Future?" (9024) , *Encounter,* Vol. 37,
no. 5 (Nov 71), pp. 19-28. Nisbet attacks the naively determinist views of
"futurologists" who imagine that extrapolation of the recent past will be
reliable guide to the future of human societies. He attributes this notion to
the influence of a metaphor of growth derived from the pre-Socratic
analogy between society and biological organisms. Time, he contends, is
an objective factor governing the growth of organisms, but a subjective
factor for our civilization, which precludes any direct correlation of units
of time to units of social change. His logic disposes of simplistic pre-
dictions in the social realm, but fails to encompass the efforts of more
sophisticated social forecasters such as Robert Theobald, who treat the

correlation of future time intervals to the magnitude of social change as contingent and open to conscious influence by those seeking to fashion their own future.

The Cultural Challenge to Science.
Theodore Roszak, ed., *Sources; An Anthology of Contemporary Materials Useful for Preserving Personal Sanity While Braving the Great Technological Wilderness* (9025) (N.Y.: Harper & Row, 1972) xxv, 572 pp., illus., register of organizations. Articles by Abraham Maslow and others describe concerns to which science has been inattentive, while collections of poems and essays illustrate themes underlying the revival of humanism: community, the whole earth, transcendance, person, and body.

CULTURAL, ART, RELIGIOUS, AND PHILOSOPHICAL INSTITUTIONS

Call to Museums to Function as Communications Institutions.
Alma Wittlin, Museums: In Search of a Usable Future (90000) (MIT Press, 1970), xiii + 300 pp., illus., $15.00. Reviewed in PROMETHEUS One/two, pp. 23-25.

Museum Accreditation.
Leaflet, 4 pp., American Association of Museums, 2233 Wisconsin Avenue, N.W., Washington, D.C. 20007. Describes procedures of the Commission on Museum Accreditation of the American Association of Museums. The museum is defined as "an organized and permanent non-profit institution, essentially educational or aesthetic in purpose, with professional staff, which owns and utilizes tangible objects, cares for them, and exhibits them to the public on some regular schedule." (90001)

Census and Program Survey of Museums.
U.S. Office of Education, *Museums and Related Institutions: A Basic Program Survey* (90002) (Washington: U.S. Government Printing Office, 1970) 0-356-574, ix + 120 pp., $1.25. National survey of museums by U.S. Office of Education, Smithsonian Institution, and American Association of Museums identifies 2,889 museums in the U.S. Categories of the survey include governing authority, age groupings of visitors, exhibit subjects (i.e., art, science, and history), educational-cultural activities, and relationships to governmental authorities and educational institutions.

Bibliography on Museums and Education.
Philip C. Ritterbush, "Museums and Media: A Basic Reference Shelf" (90003), Dec 70, 15 pp. Available from ERIC Clearinghouse on Educational Media and Technology, Institute for Communication Research, Stanford University, Stanford, California 94305. Documents growing recognition of community-based learning, with 13 general references on museums and 43 references on museum education activities. Introduction by Richard Grove.

Federal Aid to Museums.
Congressman John Brademas, Remarks in introducing the Museum Services Act authorizing federal support in the amount of $40 million per year for one-half of project costs, and text of H.R.8677, *Congressional Record,* 24 May 71 (90004).

Institutional Barriers to Effectiveness of Museums.
Jon Seeger and Samuel Rizzetta, "Some Educational Considerations Relating to Public Activities of the National Museum of Natural History" (90005), 110 pp. Available on request from the Office of the Director, National Museum of Natural History, Smithsonian Institution, Washington, D.C. 20560. Critique of the obscurity of the educational goals of museums. Proposals to place museum exhibits on a sound conceptual basis and to create opportunities for self-directed learning by visitors. Recommends institutional changes to transform museums into agencies for communication and interaction with visitors. A radical reinterpretation of the education program of the National Museum of Natural History (and anthropology, of the Smithsonian Institution.

Art Museums Judged Confining.
Gyorgy Kepes, "Toward Civic Art" (90006), *Leonardo,* Vol. 4, No. 1 (Winter 71), pp. 69-73. Art oversteps the boundaries imposed by the conventional museum setting. Neither the technological exuberance which drives some of today's art nor the desire of some artists to modify or recreate the physical environment can be contained in museums.

Challenges to Art Galleries.
Duncan F. Cameron, ed., *Are Art Galleries Obsolete?* (90007) (Toronto: Art Gallery of Ontario, 1969) 110 pp., $5.00 Report of a symposium held by the Art Gallery of Ontario in 1968. Calls for cultural cohesion and the democratization of art pose strong challenges to the conventions of art galleries. The editor, recently appointed Director of the important Brooklyn Museum, was quoted by the *New York Times* as giving the early appointment of a sociologist to be one of his strong intentions for the museum, in order to draw upon studies in social psychology and art education.

Cultural Mission of Natural History Museums.
Albert Eide Parr, "Museums in Megalopolis" (90008), *Gazette of the Canadian Museums Association,* Vol. 4, Nos. 4-5 (Aug, Nov 70), pp. 19-25. Merely to offer information about a world of nature ever more remote from the masses of city-dwellers is an obsolete task for museums, based on outdated concepts of the diffusion of knowledge. Museums should undertake to guide opinion, not simply transmit factual knowledge, thereby serving to offset the sensory impoverishment of the urban setting. The celebration of the diversity of man's biological, historical, and artistic heritage under conditions of visual immediacy is the task of all major museums, serving to eliminate subject-matter distinctions among them. Dr. Parr is Director Emeritus of American Museum of Natural History.

Museums: Their Cultural Role.
S. Dillon Ripley, *The Sacred Grove; Essays on Museums* (90009) (New York: Simon and Shuster, 1969) 159 pp., $5.00. In these graceful and urbane reflections the Secretary of the Smithsonian Institution offers some historical explanations of institutional anomalies in the world of museums. Why, for example, are some cultures treated as "primitive" and relegated, along with those who study them, to museums of natural history, while others, comparable in attainments, are studied and exhibited more worshipfully in museums of art? Ripley believes that museums must develop "a new series of responses to the selective pressures shaping our culture."

Future of Museums.
Gerhard Bott, *Das Museum der Zukunft* (90010) (Cologne: M. DuMont Schauberg, 1970) 311 pp. $4.50. Forty-three essays on the future of museums by leading European members of the museum profession, on the occasion of the 150th anniversary of the founding of the Hessiches Landesmuseum, Darmstadt.

Education: An Institutional Niche for Museums?
Eric Larrabee, ed., *Museums and Education* (90011) (Washington: Smithsonian Institution Press, 1968) vii + 251 pp., $6.50. Report of a conference.

Interpretation a Function of Museums.
Wilton S. Dillon, "Museums: Fossils No Longer" (90012) *Perspectives on Education*, Vol. 3, No. 2 (Winter 70), pp. 6-11. Interpretation of leading ideas—an institutional niche for museums in the "knowledge culture."

Effects of Institutional Setting on Perception.
Arnold Rockman, "Four Experiments in the Sociology of Aesthetics" (90013), *Leonardo*, Vol. 4 (1971), pp. 129-139.

Environmental Awareness Center.
Brandywine River Museum and Tri-County Conservancy of Brandywine, Inc., (90014) Documents on two organizations that have joined forces to work for preservation of rural amenities in the Bradywine Valley.

Financial Problems of Private Arts Institutions.
D.J.R. Bruckner, "Will Our Cultural Institutions Collapse?" (90015) *Washington Post*, 26 Oct 71.

Research and Design Institute.
P. O. Box 307, Providence, Rhode Island 02901. Documents include project lists, articles describing the Institute's work. Its statement of purpose: "Human affairs ought to promote a more meaningful existence, we suspect, in this age of affluence, enlightenment, and social progress. The Research and Design Institute has been established in the State of Rhode Island to deal with our increasingly technological environment—in human terms." (9.02901)

Experiments in Art and Technology.
Experiments in Art and Technology, *TECHNE* and other documents of E.A.T. 235 Park Avenue South, New York, New York 10003. E.A.T. is a nonprofit, tax-exempt organization which on projects devoted to participation in "the new technology" and in the contemporary arts. Now has over 5,000 members. Offers members participation in a wide range of project activity and assist artists and engineers in establishing collaborations. Subscribing membership, including four issues of *TECHNE* and other publications, $20; participating memberships without charge to artists, engineers, scientists, and other professionals who can and will actively participate in E.A.T. services and projects; sponsoring membership, $100 per year; other categories at higher sustaining rates. Among available publications are bibliographies, reports, and exhibition catalogues. (9.10003)

Participatory Networks to Refashion the Future.
Alternative Pursuits for America's Third Century. (9.92014) Worksheets and tape cassette for use in inaugurating participatory planning of institutional alternatives, produced under a grant from the National Institute of Mental Health by Conference Design, Inc., Post Office Box 861, Del Mar, California 92014.

Association for Humanistic Psychology.
(9.94114) The Association's stated interests are in transpersonal phenomena and the human potential movement. It publishes the *Journal of Humanistic Psychology*, a newsletter, and periodic listings of colleges and universities favoring humanistic approaches in psychology—this last a unique effort at evaluation of instructional programs by a society representing professional interests in change. 416 Hoffman Street, San Francisco, California 94114.

OTHER ACROPOLIS BOOKS OF SOCIAL SIGNIFICANCE

The Kidner Report

A Guide to Creative Bureaucracy
by JOHN KIDNER

112 pages, 6" x 9", charts, diagrams, illustrations, appendix, index, bibiography

Kidner takes a satirical look at the time-honored activities of bureaucrats at the paper clip and stapler level. Canons, Reports, and Administrative Papers.

Library of Congress No. 72-3814

Standard Book No. 87491-338-1 (paper)   **$5.95 cloth**
 87491-337-3 (cloth)   **$3.50 quality paper**

The United States vs. William Laite

by WILLIAM LAITE, JR.

250 pages, 6" x 9"

Bill Laite, a three-times elected Georgia State Representative and a leading local businessman, went to jail, convicted of a labor law infraction. His experiences in jail are eye-opening and horrifying—and the contrast between his two lives, as a leading citizen, and a jailed criminal, point out the close line we all walk between freedom and imprisonment.

Library of Congress No. 75-184718

Standard Book No. 0-87491-324-1   **$6.95 cloth**

Why Aren't We Getting Through?

The Urban Communication Crisis

by MONROE, VON ECKARDT, JOHNSON, SCHULBERG, ROUSE, SHOQUIST, HEISLER, GREENBERG, HOLMAN, and HANSON
Edited by Edmund M. Midura, Professor of Journalism, U. of Md.

191 pages, 6" x 9", 11 photos, index, authors' biographies

What is the role of the news media in the continuing urban crisis? Prominent journalists and community leaders take a comprehensive look at the crisis in urban communication and the problems of the mass media in its efforts to reach the inner city.

Library of Congress No. 70-148676

Standard Book No. 87491-312-8 (cloth)   **$6.95 cloth**
 87491-316-0 (paper)   **$3.95 paper**

Politics and the Press

by GALLUP, BRODER, KLEIN, RIVERS, LANG, RASPBERRY, POTTER, DILLARD, CORNWELL and CHANDLER
Edited by Richard W. Lee, Dept. of Journalism, U. of Md.

191 pages, 6" x 9", 10 photos, index, bibliography

Based on the University of Maryland Distinguished Lecture Series. Prominent Social Scientists and journalists reveal their attitude toward the public's right to know, and the role of the press with unusual candor.

Library of Congress No. 72-118670

Standard Book No. 87491-132-X (cloth)   **$6.95 cloth**
 87491-131-1 (paper)   **$3.95 paper**

Inside America

Radicalization of a Black African Diplomat
by FRED HAYFORD

256 pages, 6" x 9"

A highly placed diplomat from Ghana looks at the United States clearly and without prejudice and comes up with some startling conclusions!

Library of Congress No. 78-184716

Standard Book No. 0-87491-326-8   **$6.95 cloth**

Wall Street: Security Risk

by HURD BARUCH

356 pages, 6" x 9", charts, appendices, index

An ex-SEC lawyer levels his guns at the New York Stock Exchange and Wall Street—and finds that the small investors' funds are misused by their brokers. He reveals myriad problems on Wall Street and makes recommendations to prevent the reoccurrence of the debacle of the late 1960's.

Library of Congress No. 74-177258

Standard Book No. 0-87491-320-9   **$8.95 cloth**

The Political Image Merchants:

Strategies in the NEW POLITICS
by BRODER, NAPOLITAN, WHITE, LAURENT, SCAMMON, et al.
Edited by Ray Hiebert, Robert Jones, Ernest Lotito, and John Lorenz
Forewords by Rogers C.B. Morton, Lawrence O'Brien, Robert J. Dole

312 pages, 6" x 9", photos of authors, index, authors' biographies

Are political candidates packaged and sold like cereal and soap? This behind-the-scenes glimpse examines the activities of campaign managers, advertising agencies, pollsters, and public relations firms.

Library of Congress No. 76-148048

Standard Book No. 87491-314-4 (cloth)   **$7.95 cloth**
 87491-315-2 (paper)   **$4.95 paper**

Save Your Health and Your Money

A Doctor's Answers to Today's High Health Costs
by PATRICK J. DOYLE, M.D., Past President, American Health Foundation

240 pages, 6" x 9", index, bibliography, appendices

The author, past president of the American Health Foundation, in his new health "Bible," covers topics ranging from choosing a doctor, hospital and community services, health insurance, drugs and appliances to tax deductions for health and medical care.

Library of Congress No. 70-148049

Standard Book No. 87491-133-8 (cloth)   **$6.95 cloth**
 87491-139-7 (paper)   **$3.95 paper**

acropolis books ltd.

COLORTONE BLDG., 2400 SEVENTEENTH ST., N.W., WASHINGTON, D.C. 20009

Prometheus Original Paperbacks

94

THE BANKRUPTCY OF ACADEMIC POLICY
by Peter Caws, S. Dillon Ripley, Philip C. Ritterbush, editor

128 pages, 6'' x 9'', index, illustrations

Essays on the proper role of the University in today's society.

Library of Congress No. 72-75040

Standard Book No. 87491-500-7   **$3.95** *paper*

SCIENTIFIC INSTITUTIONS OF THE FUTURE
Philip C. Ritterbush, editor

150 pages, 6'' x 9'', index, illustrations

Essays taken from the 1971 American Association for the Advancement of Science Symposium.

Library of Congress No. 72-3811

Standard Book No. 0-87491-501-5   **$3.95** *paper*

TALENT WASTE: Institutional Malfunction in the Market for Skilled Manpower (1972)
Philip C. Ritterbush, editor

150 pages, 6'' x 9'', index, illustrations

Library of Congress No. 72-3816

Standard Book No. 0-87491-502-3   **$3.95** *paper*

THE LEARNING MACHINE:
**The Impact of Communications Technology
on Higher Education and Research (1972)
Philip C. Ritterbush, editor**

150 pages, 6'' x 9'', index, illustrations

Library of Congress No. 72-3817

Standard BookNo. 0-87491-503-1   **$3.95** *paper*

acropolis books ltd.

GENERAL BOOK BINDING CO.
212PA   625   7242
73   COLORTONE BLDG., 2400 SEVENTEENTH ST., N.W., WASHINGTON, D.C. 20009
QUALITY CONTROL MARK

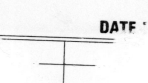

DATE